JERUSALEM
IN NEW TESTAMENT TIMES
20 B.C. ⟶ 70 A.D.

THIRD NORTH WALL ?

THIRD NORTH WALL ?

BETHESDA

SUBURB

UPPER

CITY

LOWER

CITY

0   500 1000 1500 FT.

Adventures in the Holy Land

BOOKS BY NORMAN VINCENT PEALE

Adventures in the Holy Land
The Tough-Minded Optimist
Guideposts to a Stronger Faith (*editor*)
The Amazing Results of Positive Thinking
Unlock Your Faith Power
Stay Alive All Your Life
He Was a Child
Coming of the King: The Story of the Nativity
Inspiring Messages for Daily Living
The Power of Positive Thinking for Young People
Faith Made Them Champions (*editor*)
The Guideposts Anthology (*editor*)
The Power of Positive Thinking
New Guideposts (*editor*)
Guideposts (*editor*)
The Art of Living
Not Death at All
A Guide to Confident Living

WITH DR. SMILEY BLANTON

The Art of Real Happiness
Faith Is the Answer

Adventures
in the
Holy Land

by
Norman Vincent Peale

Prentice-Hall, Inc., Englewood Cliffs, N. J.

The author wishes to thank the following publishers and authors for
permission to reprint passages from their copyrighted works:
J. B. Lippincott Company and the Institute of Current World
Affairs for *The Arab Awakening* by George Antonius, copyright 1939 by
J. B. Lippincott Company, copyright 1943 by the Institute of Current
World Affairs.
William Morrow & Company, Inc. for *The Bible as History* by
Werner Keller, © 1956 by Werner Keller.
Frederick A. Praeger, Inc. for *Digging Up Jericho* by Kathleen M.
Kenyon.
Princeton University Press for *Archaeology and the Old Testament*
by James B. Pritchard, copyright © 1958 by Princeton University Press
and *Gibeon Where the Sun Stood Still* by James B. Pritchard, copyright
© 1962 by Princeton University Press.
St. Martin's Press and Macmillan & Co., Ltd., London, for *History
of the Arabs* by Philip K. Hitti.
University of Illinois Press and Sari Jamil Nasir for *The Image of
the Arab in American Popular Culture* by Sari Jamil Nasir.

To my dear wife Ruth
whose companionship
has enriched every journey
and whose advice and assistance
in the writing of this book have been invaluable

To our beloved children
and other members of the family
whose presence has made our journeys
truly a family pilgrimage to the Holy Land

To our many cherished friends
who have accompanied us on our trips of a lifetime

This book is lovingly dedicated

Sincere appreciation is extended to the following associates who assisted in the preparation of this manuscript:
Mrs. Mary M. Creighton
Miss Winona Grant
Mrs. Doris W. Phillips
Mr. Ben Wilbur

Special appreciation to:
Arab Information Center
Consulate of Lebanon
Israel Information Services
Jordan Tourism Authority
United Nations
United Nations Relief and Works Agency for Palestine Refugees

Contents

1

The Trip of a Lifetime

I N STRANGE WAYS MY LIFE HAS BEEN DIFFERENT EVER SINCE MY FIRST
trip to the Bible Lands. Time after time I have been drawn back
to the fascinating countries at the far eastern end of the blue Mediterranean where civilization was cradled and where, on each return, I
find new and amazing personal values.

So come with me to the Holy Land where there is charm and romance
at every turning. Here in this book, through pictures and words, I want to
present to you the Holy Land as I see it and love it.

Fourteen hours from New York our jet airplane comes down the radar
beam into a different world, a fascinating world of sound and color and
throbbing life. It is a world where history lives again; where the Bible
comes dramatically alive.

The approach is over the sea. Straight ahead the glistening white buildings of Beirut, Lebanon, greatest city of the Middle East, rise tier upon
tier up the steep green hills from the shore where St. George killed the
dragon. Americans, whose newspapers have neglected this area, are astonished by this sophisticated city with its modern, many-storied apartments,
hotels and splendid business sections seen from the plane as it descends for
a landing. The airport is one of the busiest and best equipped in the
Eastern world.

On the ground you realize at once that you are in the Middle East.
Among the multitude of passengers you hear the babel of many tongues
and the plaintive and haunting music of the Orient. You feel the friendly
courtesy and obviously slower tempo. Brown hands reach for your bags,

13

That the sophistication of ancient Phoenicia continues in modern Lebanon is evidenced by its advanced hotel architecture. Every amenity provided by the best American hotels is available here.

brown faces light up with smiles, white teeth flash, and you hear for the first time words spoken in a quaint English accent you will continue to hear over all the Middle East, "You are welcome, you are welcome."

Riding into town from the airport you are amazed by the construction going on everywhere as this bustling city reaches ever outward along the sea and over the hills. That Beirut is one of the really beautiful cities of the world is immediately evident to the arriving visitor. Its incomparable beauty of situation is matched by the most striking modern architecture.

Few cities provide a more magnificent approach than that of the ride along the Rue Souleiman Boustani and into the Rue de Chouran, which skirts the deep blue Pigeon Grotto. Then we drive into the noble Avenue de Paris, a wide palm-lined boulevard that sweeps majestically along the sea, past the famous American University, and on into the heart of the town. Here, as everywhere in the Holy Land, you will experience the contrast of the new and the old. The visitor is entranced by the mystic spell of the East even before he reaches his hotel.

And what a surprise awaits you when, with that flourish only Middle Eastern drivers give to a car, you come to a dramatic stop before the modern hotel entrance.

For a moment you think a colorful Arab sheik is greeting you. Actually he is the doorman holding open a glittering glass door leading to an air-conditioned interior. You walk luxuriously on a deep red carpet to an escalator which carries you to a marble-floored lobby with charming furnishing and décor. Hardly have you reached the reception desk when a man who could be straight out of the Arabian Nights pours Turkish coffee from a long-stemmed, gleaming brass coffeepot into a china cup.

Swift elevators carry you to your floor. You walk along a wide, wall-to-wall carpeted corridor to a commodious room that equals and in many cases surpasses hotel rooms in our largest American cities. Later, on your private balcony, watching the long silvery path of the moonlight on the Mediterranean, the balmy night air lies softly around you. You are in Beirut, one of the oldest and yet most modern cities in the world. You are in the exotic Middle East. You are at the romantic gateway to the Holy Land.

The countryside of Lebanon is imposing. Villages nestle in valleys throughout the Lebanon Mountains—each village in sight of the next, like a friendly chain of communities. This is Becharreh, home town of Jebran, famous Lebanese philosopher, poet and painter. It is enroute to the famous cedars of Lebanon.

This grove of the cedars of Lebanon is high in the mountains. It is a remnant of the vast forests from which Solomon imported wood for the building of his temple in Jerusalem.

Beirut, the population of which is now well over 500,000 people, was established in the Fifteenth Century B.C., according to cuneiform writing found at Tell-el-Amarna in Egypt. Centuries later Agrippa conquered Beirut and made it a Roman colony. The Fifth Macedonian and Third Gaelic legions were stationed here. The town was named in honor of the Emperor's daughter Colonia Julia Augusta Berytus, and Beirut was granted the rights of a Roman city.

Herod the Great and succeeding emperors built magnificent structures: temples, baths and theaters; ruins of these still remain, but most were destroyed or toppled into the sea in a cataclysmic earthquake and tidal wave in A.D. 551. From this teeming port Phoenician traders sailed to every city on the Mediterranean. Beirut's law school was one of the most famous in the world. It was a center of culture and sophistication. And Christianity in its early spreading out from Jerusalem deeply penetrated the life of this city and that of the Levant.

In its long history Beirut has played an important part in great events, notably the Crusades. Under the rule of Jean of Ibelin, the "old Sire of

Beirut," its influence spread through the Latin orient. It became a great prize, to be captured finally by the Muslim Mamelukes. Lebanon, with Beirut its capital, is now a sovereign republic with a high order of culture and prosperity. The population is heterogeneous, with Arabs predominating and minorities of Druze, Kurds, Sudanese and Westerners.

Beirut boasts excellent educational institutions, chief of which is the American University, founded in 1866 by David Bliss of the American Presbyterian Mission. At the San Francisco conference which constituted the United Nations, it was said there were more leaders and delegates who had graduated from this university than from any other in the world.

There are many surprises in store for the visitor to the Holy Land and one is the discovery that Christianity took its rise in an era and area where existed a culture with a high degree of sophistication. This provided an early demonstration of the power of the teachings of Jesus to penetrate any culture of whatever intellectual status. It explains how Christianity was able to make deep inroads into Hellenistic life and thought.

Christianity was accepted by the humble, poor and illiterate "who heard Him gladly." But its power also reached the rich, the powerful and the learned. Christianity appealed irresistibly to the minds of men as well as to their hearts. Its great ability to do both—and this was vital if it was to influence the world through many centuries—was first demonstrated in the fascinating places through which our travels will now take us.

Although my friend and driver in the Arab part of the Holy Land, Mohummad A. Mughrabi, is usually smartly attired in western dress, he genially posed in Arabic costume.

2

New Light
on the Arab World

B EFORE LEAVING BEIRUT WE VISIT NEARBY BYBLOS, WHERE THE
mightiest civilizations of the ancient world, lying layer-caked one
upon the other, have been sliced through by excavations to reveal a dramatic accumulation of history. We clearly see that the area
comprising modern Lebanon and Syria was, in antiquity as in later centuries, the center of an advanced culture.

Byblos, declared by Philo to be the oldest city in Phoenicia, was an
ancient seaport and shipbuilding center of primary importance. From this
port the famous cedars of Lebanon were shipped to Egypt and to Solomon
for his Temple. Ships of Gebal (Byblos) returned from Alexandria bearing merchandise of high Egyptian culture as is indicated by objects found
in its ruins.

The cultural status of ancient Byblos is indicated by its prominence in
the manufacture of writing materials from papyrus, which was imported
from Egypt. To Byblos we owe the word "book" and "Biblion," from
which comes our word Bible. Indeed the city was referred to as "book
town" because so many manuscripts from papyrus reeds were published
there. In the Ninth Century after Christ the Greeks took over from
Cassian the letters of our alphabet.

The inhabitants of Phoenicia, it appears, were not too concerned as to
what nation exercised political authority over them so long as these foreign rulers did not interfere with their profitable commerce. As a result
the Phoenicians remained the world's chief maritime center through many
centuries of shifting political control.

18

These excavations are at Byblos, the ancient "book town" from which was derived our word *Bible*. Here unearthed remains of great civilizations lie layer-caked one upon the other. The Egyptians called Byblos "the land of the gods" due to the many deities.

We cannot really understand the Holy Land without some reference to the fact that along this coast, at the close of the Eleventh Century, came the crusaders bent upon recapturing the Holy Sepulchre of Jesus Christ from the "Infidel."

The crusaders apparently had a rather naïve side, for when they reached the Holy City they actually marched barefoot around Jerusalem, blowing horns and expecting the massive walls to fall at the trumpet blasts, as at

The Palace of Beit-Eddine is located approximately 35 miles from Beirut. It was built in 1830 of inlaid mosaic and is a mixture of Moorish and European architectures. Originally it housed all the emirs, or ruling kings, of Lebanon. Now it is the summer residential palace of the president.

Jericho. But a regular military siege proved more effective. The city capitulated and the invaders proceeded to massacre many of the defenders, over seventy thousand, according to Matthew of Edessa.

In 1187 the Frankish crusaders lost Jerusalem to the Arabs and the call of the muezzin replaced the Christian bell. At the same time, the golden cross surmounting the Dome of the Rock was torn down. This aroused such doughty western leaders as Frederick Barbarossa, Emperor of Germany, Richard I Coeur de Lion, King of England, and Philip Augustus, King of France. The several Crusades were on again, this time with all the color and romance that have glorified them in song and story. But the emphasis upon the picturesqueness of the Crusades, as viewed from several hundred years later, conveniently overlooks the blood and stench of piled-up corpses beside the citadel of Tripoli and the massacre of the Templars at Akka.

According to Philip Hitti, the historian, the influence of the crusaders was artistic, industrial and commercial rather than scientific and literary. And "In Syria they left in their wake havoc and ruin and throughout the Near East they bequeathed a legacy of ill will between Moslems and Christians that has not yet been forgotten." They left architectural beauty, however, and physical types. All along the Mediterranean coast from Jerusalem to Tripoli the ruins of noble watchtowers high on headlands jutting into the sea are silent reminders of the crusaders, as are the blue eyes and fair skin occasionally seen in the people of this region. They also left many beautiful churches and castles, some of which we will see on our tour.

We of the Western world owe a debt to the crusaders for bringing us, for example, new fruits from the Middle East such as lemons, melons and apricots—the latter for decades were known as the "plums of Damascus." Even scallions we owe to the crusaders, the name deriving from the onion of Ascalon, a Palestinian town.

In the Orient, as Hitti tells us, the crusaders acquired new tastes for spices and sweetmeats, as well as a desire for the perfumes of Arabia and for fragrant gums and incense. The sweet scents of Damascus became great favorites. Ginger, cloves and aromatic spices, together with pepper and other condiments became popular in the West through the crusaders.

But most important of all was sugar. Europeans for generations had been sweetening their foods with honey. But in Syria the crusaders became familiar with sugar cane. As a result sugar was the first great luxury introduced in the West. With it came soft drinks, candy and other fattening edibles. So perhaps we also owe our never-ending struggle with

These appealing faces of a refugee mother and child from the Khan Echih Camp near Damascus belong to just two out of the millions of displaced people in the Arab world.

avoirdupois to the crusaders and their foray into the culture of the Orient. Rugs, carpets, tapestries and fabrics such as muslin, damask, velvet, silk and satin were brought from the Arab world to Europe. Toilet articles, glass mirrors instead of polished steel, lacquers and dyestuffs also came to the West with the returning crusaders.

These facts illustrate once again the enlarging effect of travel upon our concepts and, in this instance, should serve to increase our respect for the Arab world, a section of our globe about which Westerners have in general been less than fully informed.

Indeed the average untraveled American has, it seems, a rather inadequate concept of the Arab world. Many actually think of it vaguely as a stretch of desert peopled by dark, bearded men who carry daggers in their belts and who live in tents or are always riding across the sands on camels. The Arab world has suffered from a poor press in this country and in some instances from actual misrepresentation through motion pictures and magazine stories. Sari Jamil Nasir declares:

> The Arab world of today is not the same world which is reflected in the fictional Arabian Nights. . . . In the Arab world there still are Bedouins who with their camels camp on the desert. But they constitute a living picture of the ancient past. Today automobiles, airplanes and locomotives are the standard means of transportation in these countries. Large metropolitan cities with skyscrapers stand on once barren lands. Industries that manufacture cars, steel, cement and many other commodities are run mostly by Arab specialists. . . . The proportion of university graduates in Egypt to the total population is eleven times as large as in Great Britain.

Damascus, regarded as the oldest continuously inhabited city in the world, is also a modern metropolis. Its forward-looking building program includes careful preservation of its charming old look. This photograph shows El Nasr Boulevard, one of the principal avenues.

The Bay of Jounieh lies on the coast of Lebanon, a land of dramatic beauty with its far vistas of mountains, valleys and sea.

Edward J. Byng says, "Our western picture of Islam and the Arabs is a pitiful caricature of the reality."

How did the Western misconception of the Arab world come about? One reason may have been the vast expansion of Islam which challenged and even threatened European Christendom. This probably created a fear of the Moslem who was considered the virtual enemy of Christ. This was, of course, not true, as Christ is revered in Moslem thought. The late George Antonius, chronicler of the Arab awakening, describes the enormous and far-flung Arab empire that arose in the Seventh Century B.C. and which was well on the way to dominating the world until stopped by Charlemagne at the Battle of Tours in A.D. 732. Antonius says:

> With the preaching of the Moslem faith, a process of expansion began which was destined to lead to one of the most spectacular human conquests the world has ever seen. The forces of Islam, emerging from the heart of the Peninsula shortly after the death of the Prophet Muhammad, pressed forward in every direction open to a land advance. Northwards, they overran Syria and advanced into Anatolia to threaten Constantinople. To the east, they conquered Iraq, Persia, the greater part of Afghanistan, and crossed the Oxus into what is now known as Turke-

stan. To the west, they captured Egypt, the whole of the North African coast and, reaching the shores of the Atlantic, turned northwards at Gibraltar, overran Spain and crossed the Pyrenees into France, where they occupied Avignon, Carcassonne, Narbonne and Bordeaux. In barely one hundred years from the death of Muhammad, an Arab empire had been founded which extended without a break from the Iberian Peninsula in the west, along the southern shores of the Mediterranean, to the banks of the Indus and the Aral Sea in the east. . . . Under their rule a brilliant chapter in the history of mankind was to unfold itself, and their real claim to greatness was not that they conquered such a vast portion of the known world, but that they gave it a new civilization.

Hitti tells us:

It was not only an empire that the Arabs built, but a culture as well. Heirs of the ancient civilizations that flourished on the banks of the Tigris and the Euphrates, in the land of the Nile and on the eastern shore of the Mediterranean, they likewise absorbed and assimilated the main features of the Greco-Roman culture, and subsequently acted as a medium for transmitting to medieval Europe many of those intellectual influences which awoke the Western world and set it on the road toward its modern renaissance.

No people in the Middle Ages contributed to human progress so much as did the Arabs. . . . Arab scholars were studying Aristotle when Charlemagne and his lords were learning to write their names. Scientists in Cordova, with their seventeen great libraries, one alone of which included more than 400,000 volumes, enjoyed luxurious baths at a time when washing the body was considered a dangerous custom at the University of Oxford.

Against this background of intellectuality it is rather bizarre that Americans should have the general idea that Arabs are pirates, camel drivers or belly dancers. The latter notion apparently developed from the Chicago World's Fair of 1893, as Nasir describes the circumstances: "In 1893 an Egyptian girl was credited with introducing the hootchy-kootchy dance to the United States. She later became known as Little Egypt and several films were based on this incident in which belly dancing became associated with Egypt and the Egyptians." I understand its success in the United States impelled some Arabian entrepreneurs to learn about such shows and to stage them for American tourists traveling in the Middle East.

Thus a stereotype of the Arab developed in the American mind, and was further slanted by Rudolph Valentino in a famous film called *The*

The Vocational Training Center at Siblin, Lebanon, was built by Canadian donations for the training of refugee boys. The ancient city of Sidon is in upper left.

Sheik. Valentino, who represented a phenomenon which Nasir calls "masculine sex appeal," fixed the Arab in American thought as a sort of blood-and-dagger character reveling in harems, seductions and sinister stabbings. While for the most part Arabs are pictured as villains, now and then a more objective producer has favorably emphasized the greatness of men against the desert. But as Nasir says, "The present trend on the American screen seems to present the Arab more or less favorably in historically remote situations, or in an unfavorable and unsympathetic light in contemporary situations." There have even been attempts to smear the Arabs as Nazis or at least to link them vaguely with nefarious characters of that sort.

In view of these inadequate and even ignorant concepts, it has seemed only fair to a great people to include here a brief reference to the noble civilization which Arabs have given to the world over so many centuries, including the present day.

3

Fabulous Baalbek, Tyre and Sidon

ANCIENT SOPHISTICATED CULTURE IS FASCINATINGLY REVEALED IN the ruins of Baalbek, or ancient Heliopolis ("City of the Sun"), the next objective on our tour. It is evident that there has always been a high civilization in this gateway region to the area where Jesus lived and taught. And now with the gadgetry of modern times, another high standard of civilization is coming to this part of the world.

Leaving Beirut, we mount steeply through the summer resort town of Aley, where the villas of some of the world's wealthiest people are located. We cross over the pass of Dar el Baydar at an elevation of 5,065 feet and soon there spreads out before us the far-reaching plain of Beqaa. To the west rises the famous peak Jebel Sannin, the upper slopes of which in Biblical times were covered with the cedars of Lebanon. A small, state-protected grove of cedars still remains high in the Lebanon Mountains. To the east is the Anti-Lebanon range, dominated by Mount Hermon, capped with eternal snows to which the Bible refers so feelingly.

The plain of Beqaa is a veritable Garden of Eden extraordinarily rich in agricultural products. Trucks roll daily bumper-to-bumper along smooth highways to Middle Eastern markets. As the result of its favorable climate and scientific agricultural cultivation, no valley in the Middle East is more fertile and productive.

Passing along the valley with its contrasts of tractors and camel trains, we come to Baalbek, a town of 10,000 inhabitants. Here, etched against a cloudless blue sky, is what remains of the graceful pillars of the Temple of Mercury. How those granite columns of enormous size, which undoubt-

This close-up shows the immense size and graceful detail of carving in pillars of the Temple of Jupiter Heliopolitan at Baalbek.

edly were quarried in Egypt long ago, came to stand in this inland area is not known. The manner of their transportation from the Nile Valley continues to be a speculative mystery of the ages.

Did Jesus ever visit Baalbek in person? The Gospel writers do not deal with that question. Matthew, Mark, Luke, John and Paul were not concerned with writing a diary of Jesus' daily activities, or even a general biography. They considered it more important to dwell on places and events which emphasized His message. But we know that Jesus was always on the move. Tantalizing enough, the Gospel writers record visits to only eighteen towns and villages; but surely this is only a fraction of the places He covered in His travels. We know that Jesus' mind was eagerly interested in all aspects of the life about Him. It would require only a few days

Here are some of the remaining columns of the great Temple of Jupiter Heliopolitan.

of travel for Him to visit Tyre, Sidon and Beirut. Likewise, He very well might have visited Baalbek. Surely such a fabulous place, one of the most famous sights of His world, might have called for a visit. We know that He spent some time at Tyre and Sidon, world-famous communities of His day. St. Mark tells us that Jesus ". . . went into the borders of Tyre and Sidon. . . ." (Mark 7:24)

I have found the area of Tyre and Sidon of great interest, though tourists are seldom taken there. Tyre is approximately 130 miles north from Jerusalem along the Mediterranean seacoast and, according to the record,

This interior view of the colossal Temple of Bacchus at Baalbek shows how the ancient structure is remarkably preserved.

is the farthest extent of Jesus' travels. Tyre is only 40 miles north of Capernaum, the Galilean town that was an important center in Jesus' ministry.

Tyre was the capital of the scintillating Phoenician nation. While geographically it was a small country extending about 250 miles from north to south and 15 miles at its widest point, its influence in the ancient world was out of all proportion to its size. Phoenicia was the greatest maritime nation in the world for 1,000 years. Ships of the Phoenicians were to be seen in every port of the Mediterranean, and they even passed through the pillars of Hercules into the Atlantic. The Phoenicians traded with the Scilly Isles and with Spain, and were known to have visited ports in France, England and even the Baltic Sea. Among their chief exports were the famous purple dyes of Tyre, silk and silken garments. Lucian tells how Cleopatra appeared at a banquet, arrayed in a thin-spun and clinging silk garment made by the skillful Tyrians. They were great traders and colonizers, but apparently were not interested in military domination.

At Tyre, as at Baalbek, the pagan worship of Ashtoreth and Baal featured prostitution and other evils which must have constituted a challenge to that great Teacher of pure religion who was preaching and healing only a short distance down the coast. He would certainly feel that His message of salvation should be preached to these vigorous and world-minded people to the north.

As I have driven along the Levantine coast road on my various trips, I have wondered where it was that Jesus met the Canaanite woman who lived in Phoenicia and who had a daughter "vexed with a devil." This story indicated that the reputation of Jesus had preceded Him to the northern country, for she persistently implored the Master to heal her child. Both Matthew and Mark reveal a kind of narrow provincialism, it seems to me, in urging that Jesus should not respond to her pleas on the ground that He was sent by God only to the Jews. Yet they go on to say that later He returned to Galilee where He healed all the multitude freely. But the woman of Phoenicia persisted and so received healing for her daughter. Jesus taught one of His great lessons when He said to this determined lady, "O woman, great is thy faith: be it unto thee even as thou wilt." (Matt. 15:28)

My family and I spent one sunny afternoon at Tyre contemplating the life of that once great city in the long-gone centuries. It was founded in the Fourteenth Century b.c. and was built both upon the mainland and an offshore island. A causeway was constructed by Hiram I, King of Tyre, the famous monarch who supplied Solomon with labor and material for the building of the Temple in Jerusalem. From this island fortress, Tyre, mistress of the seas, was able to defy the might of the colossal empires of Assyria and Babylonia. It successfully endured sieges by such mighty rulers as Shalmaneser III, Ashurbanipal and Nebuchadnezzar. The last actually besieged it for 13 years.

Tyre figures in the life of St. Paul, who spent a week in this teeming maritime city on his journey from Ephesus to Jerusalem while his ship "unloaded her burden"—his quaint phrase for freight handling. Many evidences of the crusaders are to be found in this area. Having captured Tyre in 1124, they made it one of the chief cities in their Kingdom of Jerusalem.

The city was taken by Alexander the Great because it stood in the way of Egypt, his main target, and it failed to deny harbor facilities to the Persian fleet after he had defeated Darius at the battle of Issus in 333 B.C. Tyre refused his request, as it was allied with Persia. It required a ganging up of a number of nations to take the island-city fortress, from which were hurled pots of burning naphtha and sulphur and red-hot sand at the enemy. But Tyre fell because Alexander used mobile siege towers 160 feet high (about 20 stories). They carried bowmen and artillery on the various levels. They were the highest siege towers in the history of war, according to Werner Keller. Scaling the walls after an 8-month siege, Alexander slaughtered 10,000 citizens and sold 30,000 into slavery. But despite these adversities Tyre recovered and was again one of the world's great cities until the Muslims destroyed it after the fall of the crusader city of Saint-Jean-d'Acre in A.D. 1291.

History indeed surrounds one as he broods on the ruins of the great mall where Alexander placed his engines of war in the long-ago, and one can imagine St. Paul walking among the throngs and telling them the good news of Jesus, Saviour of mankind. It is clear from Acts 21:3-7 that Paul found a considerable number of disciples here. He remained with them for a week and when he departed "they all brought us on our way, with wives and children, till we were out of the city: and we kneeled down on the shore and prayed."

Sidon also reeks with history. Now a city of 10,000 inhabitants, it was once a principal Mediterranean center. The skill of its artisans was immortalized by Homer. Assyria, Babylonia and Persia in turn looted the wealth of Sidon. Unlike Tyre, Sidon submitted to Alexander without resistance. It was destroyed and rebuilt a number of times and indeed was a military objective as late as the British bombardment of 1918. And among all those great happenings surely the greatest was that Jesus of

The Castle of the Sea, at Sidon, was built by the crusaders about A.D. 1228. It withstood the strong blows of the Saracens in 1253, but was abandoned in 1291 after the capture of Acre. The castle stands on an islet at the mouth of the harbor and was at one time joined to the land by a causeway.

Nazareth once walked this very ground upon which we stand—His voice preaching the gospel of salvation we can still hear clearly over the wrecks of time.

But though Jesus visited Tyre and Sidon and knew the Phoenician coast well, we can only speculate as to whether He ever actually stood within the amazing confines of Baalbek. But even so the faith which He established did go there, and eventually it undermined the pagan and licentious religions that flourished amidst the colossal temples of Baalbek. Indeed His teachings of righteousness acted finally as a kind of atomic blast which tumbled down this once mighty center some three centuries after He came into this world.

And tumbling down such a place was quite a feat, for the average size of the foundation stones of the huge temples are over 30 feet by 13 by 10 feet. Three enormous stones that supported the enclosure walls are each over 64 feet long, 14 feet high and 12 feet wide. Each of these blocks weighs approximately 750 tons. Certainly this was no primitive or nomadic civilization. Archaeologists have long debated the method by which such vast stones were cut, erected into columns and transported to Baalbek to be made into a glory that lingers today in these ruins. Indeed the Baalbek temples of Jupiter Heliopolitan, Venus and Mercury were considered the most sumptuous and grandiose of the Roman Empire.

The name Baalbek means "lord of the Beka" (Ba al Beka), and apparently does not refer to the Biblical city of Baal, according to Professor George Haddad of the University of Damascus. The date of its establishment is unknown, probably being founded by the Canaanites, who were known to the Greeks as Phoenicians. Professor Haddad states:

> Traditions and legends have connected Baalbek with old Biblical figures. These traditions mention that Adam inhabited Damascus and died not far from Baalbek; that Cain built Baalbek as a refuge; that Noah was buried in Karak Nuh south of Baalbek; that Nimrod, who built the tower of Babylon to defy Jehovah, also made the giants build the towers of Baalbek, that Abraham inhabited it for some time. Some have thought that Baalath built by Solomon in the wilderness, according to I Kings 9:18, is Baalbek, and that Solomon built a temple for Baal in this city to please his concubines and that he gave the citadel of Baalbek as a present to Balqis, Queen of Sheba.

Whatever the origins of Baalbek, we do know that Roman emperors embellished and added to its grandeur until the reign of Constantine, under whom Christianity triumphed. The licentious practices of worship carried on in honor of Venus, Goddess of Beauty and Love, were acknowledged to be inconsistent with the standards of Christ, as were also the ceremonies conducted in the Temple of Bacchus. Accordingly Constantine ordered the destruction of these temples to stamp out the debauchery connected with the worship of the Greek deities. Under Theodosius (379–395) churches were built on the sites of destroyed pagan temples, or in some cases temples were converted to churches.

Here is the approach to the Temple of Bacchus, one of the enormous shrines of Baalbek.

While the grandeur of Baalbek stirs the imagination, its principal appeal to us is that the civilizations that created it and added to its glory represented a culture challenge to Christianity. The new religion accepted and successfully met this challenge.

So, too, may culture of our own modern era—in many ways identifiable with the sophistication of those ancient times—be penetrated spiritually. Christianity has proved its ability to identify with and be at home in any age and culture, and to provide effective answers for any age and for all people.

4

Damascus,
Fabled City of Color
and Romance

IT IS A STORIED COUNTRY WE NOW TRAVERSE ON OUR WAY THROUGH
Lebanon and Syria to Damascus, one of the oldest continuously
inhabited cities of mankind. I have come upon it both by air and
by motor car, but the latter is by far the most rewarding. Over these roads
have passed armies of the great conquerors. Along this way came spice- and
silk-laden caravans from the East into Damascus, fabled city of color and
romance.

We come over the Anti-Lebanon mountain range across a vast plateau,
dropping gently until we see Damascus lying among green trees and grass
and rich vegetation in the bottom of a cup surrounded by hills. It lies at
the base of Mount Kassioun on the edge of the great Oasis of Ghouta, pur-
ported to be the legendary Garden of Eden—a legend given further cre-
dence by the location of Abel's tomb on the top of a rocky hill overlooking the Baradah valley.

This Syrian city was historic long before Abraham came on his way
around the Fertile Crescent from Canaan. And what is the "Fertile
Crescent"? I like the description of it with which Werner Keller opens
his fine book, *The Bible As History*.

> If we draw a line from Egypt through the Mediterranean lands of
> Palestine and Syria, then, following the Tigris and Euphrates, through
> Mesopotamia to the Persian Gulf, the result is an unmistakable crescent.
> Four thousand years ago this mighty semicircle around the Arabian
> Desert, which is called the "Fertile Crescent," embraced a multiplicity
> of civilizations lying side by side like a lustrous string of pearls. Rays of

34

light streamed out from them into the surrounding darkness of mankind. Here lay the center of civilization from the Stone Age right up to the golden age of Greco-Roman culture.

The city was built here in the misty past when weary travelers, toiling across the burning desert sands, gratefully found this charming oasis. Here cool waters flowed and grapes, bananas, figs, apricots and other life-giving fruit grew in abundance as they do today. The city that developed amidst this richness became one of the greatest commercial centers of all time. Its famous bazaars, such as the Souk Hamidieh, stocked with the riches of the Orient, were eagerly visited for silks, brocades, Damascus blades, mother-of-pearl inlay and other items of exotic merchandise.

Perhaps the fact that Damascus was always chiefly a center of trade rather than politics accounts for its survival, while its ancient rivals, Babylon, Nineveh, Ur of the Chaldees and Baghdad, have long since been buried in the desert sands. Indeed the great empires that captured and ruled Damascus from time to time have themselves crumbled into rubble.

As the "port of the desert" Damascus was too important in the exchange of goods to follow other cities into oblivion. Motor and air transport today bring merchandise to Damascus, even as in centuries past camel caravans from Arabia and Persia and Egypt plodded across the desert to this oasis.

At this place in the ancient wall of Damascus, Paul was let down in a basket to escape his enemies who lay in wait for him at the gates.

A Damascus street vendor offers a delectable drink called *sus*, made from the essence of the locust bean (of the same type which John the Baptist ate in the wilderness). Note the beautiful and elaborate brass vessel from which the drink is poured.

The picturesque bazaars of Damascus are covered with lattice-work roofs through which the sun filters, casting shafts of broken light across the busy scene. Fascinating shops line the way, forming a kaleidoscope display of merchandise from Orient and Occident. Unbelievable as it may seem, nearly any type of American product may be purchased in these markets. Almost any item available in a modern drugstore or supermarket in the United States is there if you search.

One wonders if Damascus ever sleeps. Throngs surge through the bazaars and streets—except women, who are not abroad in the evening hours. In these bazaars some of the world's most skillful artisans, working in their little shops, hammer out lovely articles in brass or produce finest quality mother-of-pearl and ivory inlay. Here also are made fabulous silk brocades, fabrics interwoven with gold and silver threads that never tarnish. Indeed the words "damask" and "Damascene," expressive of quality merchandise, originated here. Other artisans create the finely tempered steel blades that became the swords and daggers of Damascus, without which, in the old days, no gentleman would venture forth. They were considered priceless by military men under both the cross and the crescent.

A street scene in a Damascus bazaar, as viewed through Roman arches, includes a dome and minaret of the Mosque of El-Tekiyeh.

The passing throngs on Damascus streets are picturesque and fascinating in their intermingling of the old and new. People in Eastern and Western dress, veiled women, bearded Bedouins, rich merchants flawlessly attired in burnooses mingle in the crowded scene. Women in fashionable Western dress and men in the latest styles of Europe and America are also seen in considerable numbers.

The exotic aroma of hot Turkish coffee blends with the fragrance of spices and foods. Arabs love the appealing sweets offered in shop after shop and patronize street vendors who sell a delectable drink called *sus*, made from the essence of the locust bean. It is poured from an elaborate, gleaming brass vessel strapped to the vendor's back. The bean from which the *sus* drink is distilled is the same nourishment, along with wild honey, that was taken by John the Baptist in the Wilderness of Judea.

But Damascus is more than a picture postcard out of the romantic past. Its wide boulevards, fine hotels, tall office buildings and stylish shops mark this, the world's oldest community, as a modern city very much a part of present-day life.

Ancient Roman arches in Damascus have been excavated and raised to the present street level.

Most important to us is the fact that one of the most stirring and important events in all Christian history occurred in the environs of Damascus—the conversion of the vigorous anti-Christian persecutor, Saul of Tarsus. On an elevation outside the city on the Jerusalem road, the great light burst overwhelmingly upon his mind. From a violent persecutor he became Christianity's greatest exponent; indeed, the chief developer of the faith he had sought to exterminate.

Saul of Tarsus, even as a young man, was extraordinarily brilliant and restlessly aggressive. Trained under the eminent teacher Gamaliel, his remarkable gifts of mind and personality so impressed Jewish leaders that, young as he was, he was made a member of the Sanhedrin which ruled the Judaistic community.

These men believed they had killed Jesus on the cross and therefore had effectively crushed His spiritual movement. But it was not long until they became uncomfortably aware that the city of Jerusalem was honeycombed with dedicated disciples of the Nazarene, convinced that their Master had risen from the dead and had commissioned them to spread the faith. Their dedication and evangelizing zeal knew no bounds. They were gaining many converts. The movement was growing, and so the Sanhedrin were determined to stamp out this persistent and resurgent faith by whatever methods seemed necessary.

Thus began a ruthless and bloody persecution, climaxed by the cruel stoning to death of one of the noblest and most attractive of Christians, a young man named Stephen, who might have equaled Paul and Peter themselves in leadership ability, judging by his elevated character and by the great speech he made to the Jewish leaders. Not able to meet his cogent arguments, and looking for an excuse to destroy him, the hate-filled mob, spurred on by its leaders, fell upon Stephen with stones, beating out his life in a rain of rocks. As he died, it is said, a radiance came upon his face. Like his Master Who was Himself murdered, Stephen was heard to say, "Lord, lay not this sin to their charge." (Acts 7:60)

Saul of Tarsus was very much a party to this despicable event. Whether he actually hurled a stone is not recorded; but the Bible clearly points out that he participated as an accessory, in that he watched the coats of those who did the murdering. Like all phony leaders he, in effect, encouraged others to do the actual dirty work, thereby rationalizing that his own hands were clean.

The powerful speech and noble death of Stephen seem to have had no salutary effect upon Saul. Indeed his anger against the Christians increased so that he literally breathed out "threatenings and slaughter against the disciples of the Lord." (Acts 9:1) He went from house to house ruthlessly rooting out Christians, both men and women, herding them into prison. The Book of Acts graphically appraises his efforts in the simple statement, "he made havoc of the church." (Acts 8:3)

But even this insatiable lust and sadistic hatred did not satisfy Saul's implacable hostility. So he went to the High Priest and asked authority to go to Damascus to break up a strong nucleus of these Jesus-followers that had developed there. He told the cunning and unscrupulous religious leader that he would bring them bound to Jerusalem and throw them into jail along with the others. The High Priest liked the young firebrand and admiringly sent him on his way to persecute the disciples of Jesus in the Syrian city.

But in the life of the spirit one never knows when God, Who has His own ways of reasoning and doing, may put His finger upon even the most unlikely man. Who could have imagined the astonishing phenomenon that was to happen? Saul boasted to his companions, as they traveled, of all that he was going to do to these Jesus-followers in Damascus, and delighted in their admiration of him as a ruthless persecutor. As they neared their destination, the ancient city came into view some eight or ten miles away, lying below in its green oasis. Around Saul and his party were only the barren hills of the desert. They eagerly urged on their donkeys and increased their pace, anxious to get at the persecuting for which the trip had been taken. But God had had enough. The moment for the great change had come. One of the world's tremendous events was to take place on that dusty road.

What the thought processes of this brilliant young man could have been we can only dimly imagine. Such restless aggressiveness could, of course, indicate inner conflict. The very violence of his efforts may have been unconsciously motivated by a deep spiritual prodding which he would not admit even to himself. Who knows? But at any rate, suddenly a light brighter than the sun and overwhelming in intensity burst upon him out of Heaven. So strong was the light that he was blinded. Stunned, he fell to the earth. A voice spoke to him clearly and distinctly: "Saul, Saul, why persecutest thou me?" (Acts 9:4) The young persecutor knew instinctively whose voice it was that asked this searching question. But even so Saul dodged. "Who art thou, Lord?" he asked, though the question itself indicated that he realized it was God talking to him, bringing him up short. Clear and distinct came the answer: "I am Jesus whom thou persecutest." Then the Lord reminded him how hard it is to rebel against one's deeper mind and conscience.

Immediately Saul became tractable and ready to be directed. Humbly he asked what the Lord wanted him to do. No longer would he rebel, no longer would he hunt down people who followed Christ. His struggle with his inner guilt ceased. He put himself completely into the Lord's hands. And the Lord simply directed him to arise and go into the city where he would be told what to do.

Saul's companions were amazed and stood speechless, hearing a voice but seeing no one. Saul obediently stood up and opened his eyes, but was so blinded that he could not see. What a change! The young zealot who had breathed out threats when he had departed from Jerusalem was now led by the hand like a child, humble and docile, into his destination, the city of Damascus. In this astonishing manner began the greatest of all careers of Christian service in the long history of the faith.

So it was that in Damascus the first dramatic events in the spiritual life of the great apostle took place. Saul remained sightless for three days and took neither food nor drink. Then the Lord spoke to Ananias, a disciple living in Damascus, telling him to go into the street called Straight (which even today is perhaps the greatest bazaar thoroughfare) and in the house of Judas he would find one Saul of Tarsus. Furthermore, Ananias was told that Saul had been praying and in his prayer had "seen" Ananias in a vision coming and putting his hand upon him, and that this act would restore his sight.

Ananias was shocked by this directive and remonstrated by reminding the Lord of all the evil this man Saul had done and intended doing also in Damascus. But the Lord told Ananias that He had chosen Saul to be His representative in carrying His Gospel both to Israel and to the Gentiles. Ananias could not have been more astonished, but faithful man that he was, who was he not to obey? He went to the indicated house, found the blinded Saul and, putting his hands upon him, said, "Brother Saul, the Lord, even Jesus, that appeared unto thee in the way as thou camest, hath

This chapel is on the site of the house of Ananias in Damascus. He was commanded by the Lord to go to the street called "Straight" and to lay his hand upon the blinded Saul of Tarsus to restore his sight.

sent me, that thou mightest receive thy sight, and be filled with the Holy Ghost." (Acts 9:17) Immediately Saul received his sight and at once was baptized into the faith he had come to persecute.

With considerable misgiving the disciples received Saul into their fellowship and instructed him in the faith. He must have been an excellent pupil and filled indeed "with the Holy Ghost," for only a few days later he was effectively preaching Jesus Christ as the Son of God. The disciples could scarcely adjust to the tremendous change in this man who had come with the avowed intent of destroying the faith which he now preached with equal zest.

As for the Jews, they were so confounded by it all and annoyed, too, that they began to figure how they could kill this man who came to kill, but was now an ardent defender of the hated faith. But the disciples were not going to let this fate happen to their brilliant young brother. So, instead of allowing him to depart by the city gates where they knew the Jews lay in wait to kill him, they ingeniously let Saul down over the wall in a basket in the dead of night and he made his escape.

Returning to Jerusalem Saul did not report to the High Priest, but rather to the disciples of Christ in that city. At first they were suspicious and afraid of him, remembering very well his former hostility. But Barnabas became convinced of the validity of the change that had taken place in him, being impressed by reports of his courageous stand for Christ in Damascus. Saul told the disciples the amazing story of all that had happened to him and they accepted him fully. In Jerusalem he spoke so boldly for Jesus that again his life was sought. Therefore, for his protection the disciples brought him to the seacoast town of Caesarea, from which he departed by ship for his old home of Tarsus.

As you meditate on this dramatic story centering in the ancient city of Damascus, walk thoughtfully down the street called Straight to the house of Ananias. Here, long before you, came Saul of Tarsus, later called Paul, and much later St. Paul. Look wonderingly upon the centuries-old city wall over which he was let down by basket in the dead of night. Through the night shadows gaze across the desert over which he disappeared in the direction of Caesarea, to begin those amazing journeys that helped build the Christian church. Finally, at the spot where Saul saw the great light out of Heaven, pray for a new vision for your own life. The world desperately needs a few modern St. Pauls. A few people of such deep dedication and flaming zeal could actually transform the life of mankind. And the light that St. Paul saw and the voice he heard can come to anyone anywhere whose heart reaches for it.

5

Deeper into the Holy Land

I
T IS ALWAYS WITH MOUNTING EXCITEMENT THAT WE SET OUR COURSE
from Damascus south-by-west for Jerusalem and all Judea. Getting
an early start, we quickly mount to higher ground, passing by
the area where Saul of Tarsus saw the great light. Then we strike off
across the desert, speeding along on smooth highways.

Overland travel was a rugged enterprise when I first traversed this terrain.
The roads were narrow and very rough, making progress slow and tedious.
A full day was required, from early morning until evening, to drive from
Damascus to Amman, capital of Jordan; and it was advisable, perhaps even
necessary, to remain there overnight before continuing to Jerusalem. We
always fortified ourselves against the heat during the slow hard journey by
carrying thermos bottles of water. Dehydration created a rather acute thirst
problem.

But on my most recent visit I was surprised at the ease of this motor trip.
It had been several years since I last drove over the area, having more recently used air transportation. The motor trip now seems speedy and com-
fortable, and one can easily reach Amman for lunch. It is no problem to see
the major sights enroute and arrive in Jerusalem for dinner. And as for cold
drinks, the inevitable and delicious bottled "Fresh-Up" is available at
refreshment stands all along the way. No longer need one suffer from thirst
while crossing this desert.

In fact, I use the word desert with lessened emphasis, for even the landscape seems to have changed. The acreage under cultivation has increased
remarkably. I was greatly impressed on my most recent trip by the amount

Four modes of transportation: donkey, human feet, camel and automobile, are apparent in this street scene in Sebaste, the ancient city of Samaria.

of cattle, sheep and goats and the ever-increasing number of tractors one sees in the fields. True, we did observe a few camel trains; and for this I am glad, as one regrets having all the flavor of an ancient and romantic past fade in the face of advancing modernity.

But there are still plenty of colorful sights to observe along the route. For example, at the border stations between Syria and Jordan we see long, sleek Cadillacs occupied by white-garbed sheiks who seem to roll luxuriously from one sumptuous home to another. It is oil, liquid gold from under the sands, that has lifted these swarthy sons of the desert to opulence, and it is oil that may ultimately lift the entire Arab world into a richer life for all.

Oil and water are the key words as we consider the future of this vast area of the earth's surface and of the more than one hundred million Arabs who live there. For our good and for theirs, and indeed for the peace of the world, let us hope that Americans may always dwell in friendship with the Arabs. This rapidly developing area represents an enormous power potential in the world's life, and this fact is all too little understood in the United States.

From Syria we cross into the Hashemite Kingdom of Jordan, in which are found most of the sacred shrines of Christianity, including, among others, Bethlehem, Jericho, Hebron (where Abraham, Isaac and Jacob are buried), the city of Samaria, Shechem, Jacob's Well, the Mount of Olives, Bethany, Gethsemane and the ancient walled city of Jerusalem, the holiest in Christendom. Jordan is a nation containing approximately 37,500 square miles, about the size of the state of Indiana. This land became an independent political entity as a result of events following the two world wars, but it was not until after World War II that its present boundaries were established and full independence gained.

Jordan is an Arab country. Arabs have been living here since long before the Christian era, and have been for all these many centuries the dominant people. Except for the period of the Crusades (1099-1187), the area now comprising Jordan and also Israel remained under Arab rule until the beginning of the Sixteenth Century. Then for four hundred years this large territory was a tenuously held and lightly administered province of the Ottoman Empire. Much earlier it had been a vaguely defined southern area of Syria under a succession of rulers: Greek, Roman and finally Arab.

Actually, there are two basic sections of Jordan: the east bank and the west bank. The east bank, or Trans-Jordan in Biblical times, was in general composed of the states of Gilead, Ammon, Moab and Edom. In fact, the name of the present capital, Amman, seems to refer to the ancient Ammon or home of the Ammonites. The west bank encompasses Judea and Samaria in which are located Jerusalem, Bethlehem, Hebron, to mention only a few of the notable Biblical places, and such important towns as Nablus (near ancient Shechem and Sychar), Ramallah and other thriving communities.

Many great nations have ruled in this area: Canaanites, Jebusites, Assyrians, Chaldeans, Persians. Alexander the Great conquered these parts in 333 B.C., while the Egyptian Ptolemies held sway in the south. It was one of these rulers, Philadelphus (284-246 B.C.), who adorned and enhanced the town of Rabbath-ammon to such an extent that he renamed it in honor of himself, calling it Philadelphia, by which it was known for centuries until in modern times it was renamed Amman. It is today a bustling and growing city of over 250,000 people and contains many splendid public buildings and charming residences.

On the heights above the city stands the palace in which are the offices of King Hussein, a young man who is a fitting successor to his grandfather, the great King Abdullah, one of the strongest monarchs of his dynasty. The young King is respected and beloved by his subjects for his keenness of mind, his courage in the face of grave danger and his strong leadership. The King mingles democratically with his people and charms them, I believe, by his dash and verve as a pilot of airplanes and driver of fast cars. He has a keen social sense and is potentially one of the greatest of Arab leaders. He possesses a strong religious faith (Islam) and has inaugurated a mosque-building campaign so that in every village a minaret proclaims faith in God. "God is our strongest security against Communism," says His Majesty.

On the hills above and behind the palace of the King was enacted a sad drama which sullied the fame of King David. It was here that he contrived to put Uriah the Hittite in the forefront of battle to assure his death so that the King might take Uriah's wife, Bath-sheba.

While resting on the roof of his palace David had noticed this woman in her nearby garden and was enamored by her beauty. Unknown to Bath-sheba David watched her from a distance as she bathed. His lust knew no bounds, so to his adulterous desires he added virtual murder. This man whom God loved could be very strong and very noble, but as this event demonstrated he could also commit sin in depth. There was in him, as in all men, the basic battle between good and evil, but to the Shepherd King's credit may it be said that the good in his life greatly outbalanced the evil. Otherwise we would never have had those moving Psalms in which is immortalized victory through God in the everlasting struggle between good and evil in the hearts of men.

In Amman, as in all cities of the Middle East, the new blends charmingly with the old. The ancient and patient camel pads softly by gleaming modern buildings. Automobile horns blare amidst bleating herds of sheep and goats being driven along the streets to market. Passing through narrow old bazaars one comes out into broad, tree-lined avenues lined with sumptuous residences.

This city has had a notable past, especially in the Roman period when in 63 B.C. it became one of the cities of the Decapolis. That league of ten cities under Roman protection was part of the Pax Romana, a vast outreach of ordered civilization that distinguished the administrative genius of Rome. Philadelphia, as it was then called, greatly flourished during this period, as is evidenced by the large theater yet remaining which was capable of seating some 6,000 people. The odeum, nymphaeum, a great temple to Hercules and a forum (now housing the national collection of antiquities), as well as the ruins of an interesting Sassanian pavilion, all attest to the affluence of the Roman city that preceded by centuries this fine modern capital.

Philadelphia enjoyed a brief revival under the Umayyad Arabs in the Eighth Century after Christ, but when the Arab capital moved from Damascus to Baghdad in the Tenth Century the entire area fell into neglect, and throughout the Middle Ages it was hardly more than an unimportant town. In 1922, however, Amman became the capital of Trans-Jordan and in 1950 the capital of the Hashemite Kingdom of Jordan, and has once again emerged as an important city of the Mediterranean world.

Jordan is a fascinating land wherein are found magnificent Greco-Roman ruins; splendid Arab palaces, lonely and aloof in the desert; majestic crusader forts and castles, and massive Turkish mosques. Jordan has a wide variety of landscape. The country is a photographer's delight. The imposing grandeur of the mountain regions, the depth and width of its valleys, the exuberant vegetation, the mystic desert areas constitute exotic scenery that is a veritable wonderland of beauty.

The climate is typically Mediterranean. There is a rainy season from November to March, when the hills and valleys are carpeted with flowers and the air is crisp and clear. Winter often brings snow to the mountains.

In Jerusalem, Jordan, the photographer patiently awaited an opportunity to get a picture in which no person in western dress appeared.

Such camel trains may be seen everywhere in the Middle East. They sometimes
consist of up to fifteen or twenty camels. Note that they walk inside the fields,
perhaps to escape speeding motor traffic on the adjoining highway.

The winter season is followed by a dry summer period, which is not unpleasant because the heat is coupled with low humidity.

For years I had avoided visiting the lands of the Bible because I could
get away only in the summertime and the wiseacres, always eager to display
their wisdom or lack of it, had solemnly warned, "Oh no, don't go to the
Holy Land in the summertime. You could never endure the heat."

I fell for this false statement for a good many years, assuming that
these people knew the facts; but finally I decided to go, regardless, and discovered that it just isn't so. Since then the same type of people have urged
me not to go to other places because "it's too insufferably hot" or "the
food isn't good" or "the water will make you sick," and forthwith I have
gone and found the heat not too bad, the food very good indeed and the
water fine. I have never had a sick day in all my travels.

There are some hot places, of course. But the Middle East, with the
exception perhaps of the Tel Aviv area, has a dry heat with low humidity,
and when you are out of the direct sun and in the shade it is not at all
unpleasant. In fact, I have felt a definite health-giving effect in the dry
heat of the Syrian desert and in the wilderness of Judea. (Incidentally,
this part of Judea isn't likely to be a wilderness too much longer, for the
desert is blossoming as the rose.) As to heat, if there are places on earth
more uncomfortable than some American cities in the summer season, I've
never seen them.

I came down from Jerusalem, Jordan, one noonday to meet a party of
Americans at the Dead Sea Hotel, a magnificent hostelry on the shore of
that vast body of water shimmering in the 100° heat. They had driven
since early morning from Damascus and were hot and tired. I greeted them
with the cheering information that they would sleep under blankets that
night in Jerusalem. Polite doubt was written on their faces. But at twilight, winding up the beautiful highway that climbs into the Judean hills,
we felt the delicious coolness. Glorious pastel colors illuminated the

mountains of Judea in a mystic light which surely is out of this world. I have beheld this extraordinary and dramatic miracle of nature in no other place I have visited. Perhaps God sends this long and fleeting shaft of light from the heavens at twilight to remind man of the glory He once sent to this famed spot on earth.

In the drive up to Jerusalem you climb from approximately 1,300 feet below sea level to 2,800 feet above sea level in a distance of 25 miles.

After dinner, sitting cool and content in the courtyard of the American Colony Hotel, listening to the music of the fountain and watching the stately pine trees pointing to the bright stars above, the heat was forgotten. Thirsts had been quenched by cold pure water from earthen pitchers set in earthen bowls of water in the rooms. The use of earthen pitchers and bowls is an ancient way of cooling water and is very effective in keeping it cool and fresh. Deep sleep came early, and as promised everyone did indeed sleep under a blanket.

Not go to the Holy Land in the summertime? How foolish can one get? Personally I believe you should go any time that you can get away and are able to scrape up the necessary wherewithal for an airplane ticket.

There is something about travel in this land of Jordan that exerts a strange fascination upon the pilgrim. Though modernization and development are increasingly evident, there still broods over all the charm and mystery of the East. The romance and glory of great events seem to tremble in the very air of these storied mountains and desert. Everywhere are those sacred footprints in which we humble pilgrims seek to walk.

Here, workers separate the wheat from the "chaff which the wind driveth away." (Psalm 1:4)

6

Jerash,
Pillared City
of Vanished Dreams

HERE IS A SORT OF CHARMING INCONSISTENCY THAT IS A CHARAC-
teristic of the Holy Land and indeed of the whole Middle East.
The unexpected bursts forth from the expected, and lends continuous surprise to travel in the romantic lands of the Bible.

On the trip across the desert from Damascus to the Dead Sea, suddenly
against the blue sky appear graceful and lovely Grecian pillars, lonely and
ghostlike. Noble Roman arches tower against desert sands. A vast and
empty theater stands against barren hills. It is Jerash (ancient Gerasa),
pillared city of vanished dreams.

This may have been the site of Ramoth-Gilead. Iamblichus believed it
was colonized by veterans of Alexander the Great. Josephus tells us that it
was captured by Jannaeus in 83 B.C. and rebuilt by the Romans. Ultimately
it was destroyed by the Jews, perhaps by Christians, too, for churches were
evidently built in some instances over pagan temples. Other destruction
followed by Vespasian's Captain Annius. But the basic cause of the city's
decay was due to changing climatic conditions, political vicissitudes and
seismic disturbances.

The dramatic ruins of Jerash mark one of the great cities of the ancient
Decapolis, or 10-city league. It lies northward some 35 miles from Amman.
Here we have one of the most complete examples in existence of a Roman
provincial city, one that leaves upon the traveler's mind an unforgettable
impression of grandeur.

"The city of a thousand columns," one writer has called this once important metropolis lying on the desert's edge in an oasis of the golden river.

50

Street in Jerash (Gerasa of the Bible), once lined by magnificent structures, still shows ruts worn in the paving stones by traffic. Along this street ruins of shops are visible.

Madeleine Miller calls it "the Pompeii of the East." Indeed its rows of imperial columns, casting long shadows over chariot-rutted paving stones, are reminiscent of that tragic city under the heights of Vesuvius.

That our Lord was well known in Jerash is indicated in St. Matthew (4:25): "And there followed him great multitudes of people from Galilee, and from Decapolis, and from Jerusalem, and from Judaea, and from beyond Jordan." Even the sophisticated citizens of the provincial cities, it seems, yearned toward this wonderful Teacher and Healer. For of Him it was said (Matt. 4:24): "And his fame went throughout all Syria: and they brought unto him all sick people that were taken with divers diseases and torments, and those which were possessed with devils, and those which were lunatick, and those that had the palsy; and he healed them." Evidently human need reached even from such pagan centers as the Decapolis cities to that gentle Lover of mankind Who had healing and renewal in His words and in His touch.

Here is a general view of the large oval forum and a section of the street of columns of ancient Gerasa.

St. Mark (5:1-20) tells of the mental healing of the man with the un-
clean spirit in the country of the Gadarenes, a place we shall see later when
we visit the Sea of Galilee. The restored man was so joyful and enthusiastic
that "he departed, and began to publish in Decapolis how great things
Jesus had done for him: and all men did marvel." Our map shows how far
this happy man traveled to tell the "old, old story of Jesus and His love."

Jesus knew the cities of the Decapolis well, including Gerasa, which in
the time of His earthly ministry was still being developed and adorned
with those glorious monuments that yet remain to thrill the modern Holy
Land pilgrim. St. Mark (7:31) tells us: "And again, departing from the
coasts of Tyre and Sidon, he came unto the sea of Galilee, through the
midst of the coasts [regions] of Decapolis."

The cities of the Decapolis, of which Gerasa (Jerash) was second only
in importance to Damascus, are generally thought to be Scythopolis on the
west bank of Jordan, Hippos, Gadara (on the Sea of Galilee), Pella, Philadelphia (Amman), Dion, Kanatha, Raphana and Damascus. They formed
a league of ten independent Greek cities united by trade bonds. This con-
federation probably began when Pompey granted freedom to these cities.
Their growth and development evolved mainly from the spread of Greek
influence following the conquests of Alexander the Great in the Fourth
Century B.C.

Some of the Decapolis cities were on the mountains east of the Sea of
Galilee. Others stood south of the sea near the Jordan River and some
were built high on the eastern uplands. However, all ten were on the
strategic trade routes to the Mediterranean and of course were on the
routes from Damascus and Petra of the Nabataeans. In the time of Christ
these were rich and prosperous cities enjoying a life of brilliant culture.
Foreign traffic flowing through them kept their citizens constantly in touch
with the world outside.

The roads that once linked these cities have vanished into nothingness,
save perhaps for a lonely marble pillar or a fragment of rutted pavement
protruding from the desert sands. But in the time of Christ these roads
were filled with chariots and camel trains bearing rich goods from Rome,
Alexandria, Damascus, Petra and Baghdad. Roman troops marched down
these highways and ruts worn by their chariots can yet be traced. Although
this once throbbing life has vanished in time, the impressive might and
grandeur of Jerash remain in the magnificent monuments of great antiquity.

Before reaching the walls of the ancient city (over fine highways with
which even the great roads built by the Romans could hardly compare)

we come upon the Triumphal Arch built to celebrate the visit to Jerash of Emperor Hadrian in A.D. 129. The colossal arch excavated to only half of its original height is 39 feet high, 21 feet wide and 22 feet deep. It was a gate of honor facing the principal entrance to the city and was opened only to admit great personages.

I seem to sense more historical romance among the streets, columns and temples of Jerash than in any other city of antiquity that I have visited. It is not difficult here to reconstruct life as it must have been in the long ago. This city has lain for centuries under accumulating mounds of sand, and its distance from the present centers of civilization left it relatively undisturbed. While other cities crumbled, or their stones and pillars were carted off to build modern structures, Jerash is remarkably preserved. Its magnificent theater, paved thoroughfares, baths, fountains and temples are extant. Seventy-five tall and stately pillars still line its long main street; indeed, of the 520 such pillars in Jerash, over 200 still stand.

Near the city's entrance is a large hollow in the ground where once was an artificial lake. It was here that mock naval battles delighted the crowds. Nearby was a circus, or stadium, for gladiatorial combats.

We walk into a vast circular area, a kind of forum, in which the great paving stones are perfectly laid in graceful half-arcs, the whole surrounded by a circular colonnade of 57 lovely Grecian columns. There is an elevated walking place above the street level of the forum. To me, so real is the illusion of the past that amidst the desert stillness the cries of the crowd, only yesterday dispersed by time, seem carried in the still air.

I last visited here in the late afternoon and gratefully sat for a while in the cool shade of an immense pillar. The lengthening shadows falling on the old stones of the forum endowed their surfaces with a soft patina. As the sun began to sink lower the pillars cast long shadows over the well-worn floor of the forum. I could not help wondering if among all the

This close-up of a portion of the great oval forum of Gerasa shows that many of the huge Ionic columns still carry their architrave. Over fifty such columns encircle the great open plaza in which the paving stones are laid in perfect circular form.

thousands of feet which had crossed and recrossed those stones, may not there have been those of the Master Himself? It is entirely reasonable to suppose that one who eagerly loved life and people as He did would have moved among the throngs on these streets as well as in other places specifically mentioned.

Surely when Jesus came "through the midst of the coasts [regions] of Decapolis," He did not fail to visit stately Jerash. That fine mind that was able at twelve years of age to dispute with learned doctors would certainly have fascinated the sophisticates of Jerash.

I placed my hand with reverent hesitation upon the time-weathered stone on which I was seated. The thought came that Jesus might have rested here and taught the people. Actually, there was something so real in the notion that I felt compelled to rise and move on, not accounting myself worthy to sit where He might have sat.

We moderns tend to look rather indulgently upon the ancients, regarding them as relatively primitive when compared to our own civilization. But a walk down "Main Street" in Jerash is likely to correct such a bumptious attitude. Perhaps in back streets and alleys there were poor dwelling places, but on an evening the humblest citizen might walk with his family along noble avenues and be thrilled by silvery moonlight falling upon pillared temples and public buildings, sights that would make most modern cities look drab by comparison.

Jerash, a city of the finest of Roman architecture, is an excellent example of early town planning. It even has a central traffic circle where two principal streets cross. In the center of the crossing stands a huge, well-preserved monument, a fountain in which the water system yet remains. Open manholes reveal an excellent under-street drainage system. Large niches in the masonry of the fountain once held statues of the great figures of Greece and Rome. The city was surrounded by walls 8 feet thick with a total circuit of 3,000 yards. Six gates pierced the huge walls.

This traffic circle is at an intersection of two main streets in Jerash. Great fountains containing niches for statues still stand and an under-the-street water system is revealed.

The magnificent theater of Gerasa, some of whose seats still bear their ancient numbers, is one of the most perfectly preserved theaters of the Greco-Roman world.

To get an impression of the size of the buildings of Jerash, I climbed a wide flight of some 50 steps to a massive platform from which rose the majestic Temple of Artemis (patron Goddess of Gerasa) towering high against the sky. W. F. Albright says decades must have been required to complete it. Travelers from distant hilltops must have gazed in awe upon this great edifice and others hardly less impressive.

That the cities of the Decapolis were islands of Greek culture in an alien land is borne out by the magnificent theater of Jerash, the pillars and proscenium of which are still standing. The circular seating rises tier upon tier, the whole encompassing a half-circle and embracing a stage and orchestra. I estimated a seating capacity of over 5,000 persons. Being a platform speaker myself, I tested the acoustics and found that the theater had an acute sound system in which no microphone would be at all necessary. So perfectly preserved is this Greek theater, even to seat markings, that if an ancient turned up with the proper ticket for one of the plays now staged by the Jordanian government, his seat reservation could hardly be questioned.

Late twilight had come when I took my last look at Jerash. The sinking sun sent one long beam of light against the colonnaded pillars of the forum which flashed back red and gold. Then, quickly, night came again to one of the most glorious ruins of mankind's life on this earth, and a thin crescent moon appeared in the sky.

Could I see imaginatively a tall figure surrounded by sturdy men walking along the mountainous road that strikes off toward Judea? At any rate, I was lost in thought about Him as we sped over a magnificent highway toward the Holy City of Jerusalem. I shall never forget and shall hope to return to Jerash, pillared city of vanished dreams.

7

Where
the River Jordan Flows

WE MOVE NOW INTO ONE OF THE MOST IMPRESSIVE AND SPEC-
tacular areas on earth. Here within the space of a few miles
occurred some of the greatest events in the history of mankind. Here are place names and locations famed in spiritual story, which
are well known to every reader of the Bible.

The Jordan valley, a vast fault in the earth's surface, is the lowest spot
on the globe, 1,297 feet below sea level at the Dead Sea. The Dead Sea is
approximately 1,300 feet deep, so from the top of Mount Nebo, 2,644 feet
high, where Moses stood, to the bottom of the sea is almost a perpendicu-
lar mile into the heart of the earth.

The enormous rift, of which the Jordan valley is a part, is 160 miles
long and from 2 to 15 miles wide. George Adam Smith, in his book,
The Historical Geography of the Holy Land, says, "on earth there is nothing else like this deep colossal ditch."

In this great trench winds the most famous river of all time, the river
Jordan in which our Lord was baptized and whose waters "flow" spiritually
into every Christian church the world over. The river takes its rise from
the melting snows of Mount Hermon and flows first into Lake Huleh,
thence on and into the Sea of Galilee. Then it runs for about two hundred
miles of twisting and turning through mountains and desert with a 9-foot
fall in a distance of 65 miles until it pours into the Dead Sea. Lined by
willows and tamarisks it forms a streak of green through a barren wilderness of whitish brown hills and cracked desert earth.

I have spent many days and some evenings in the Jordan valley and have
found it strangely appealing. I say "strangely," for some writers have de-

scribed this enormous gash in the earth as a most unattractive area, even using such horrifying superlatives as its "burning heat," its "suffocation," its "macabre likeness to the lunar surface of the moon" or its "dreadful desolation."

As for me, I have never seen a thermometer reading higher than 104° Fahrenheit in July and August. I have actually been disappointed in this, for some of the above-mentioned writers refer to a blast-furnace-like heat of 125°. This I would actually like to experience, but thus far the Jordan valley has failed to deliver it for me. Moreover, I have never sat on the shaded terrace of the beautiful Dead Sea Hotel that my cheeks have not been fanned by a breeze, a warm one to be sure, but never have I experienced a "dead lifeless air." It is a hot, bleached, though immensely powerful, desert region, but I love the desert and respond to its lure.

This hotel at the lowest spot on earth, 1,200 feet below sea level, is a popular winter resort area in Jordan.

As blue and sparkling as Tahoe in California, the Finger Lakes of central New York State or Lake Lucerne in Switzerland is the Dead Sea. Forty-seven miles long and ten miles wide it covers an area of 360 square miles. The Jordan pours into the Dead Sea a daily average of six million tons of water. Rainfall in the valley is approximately five inches per year. There is, of course, no outlet to this sea except by evaporation and this is actually visible at times in rather strange, blue-white clouds that float half-formed and ethereal above the waters.

Medieval travelers circulated preposterous stories about the Dead Sea, to the effect that in its "poisonous air" plants could not live, and birds flying over its "dread" waters would drop dead. They also said that no movement ever disturbed its ghostly still surface. Of course, none of this is true, nor is the lake a somber place. On the contrary, its varied effects of light and shadow, the intense and lovely coloring, the pastel shades that drift over the encompassing mountains actually produce a sublime and unforgettable beauty.

As long as I dwell on this earth I shall cherish the memory of that soft and balmy night when, awestruck, we saw a full moon sail over the mountains of Moab, sending its shaft of light over the waters. Natives as well as tourists travel miles to witness this amazing and spectacular phenomenon of nature. My family and I did just that and the glorious sight was one of the great experiences of beauty in our lives.

Dead Sea water has a rather oily feel. Ordinary salt water holds approximately 5 per cent of solids in solution, but in the Dead Sea it is perhaps 25 per cent. It is almost impossible for a bather to sink in this sea, and it is great sport to feel the sustaining quality of this water. H. V. Morton tells a story that when Titus stood by the Dead Sea in A.D. 70, he caused several slaves chained together to be thrown into the water, but they remained safely on the surface and so gained their lives. Excellent bathing facilities, as well as accommodations and entertainment, are available at the large modern Dead Sea Hotel. All rooms, incidentally, face the sea.

The central height is the Mount of Temptation, on which Jesus was tempted by the devil. The mountain towers over the Jericho plain, in which there is increasing cultivation, as the picture shows.

WHERE THE RIVER JORDAN FLOWS 59

Standing on the terrace of the hotel, you are not only in the midst of a breathtaking environment, but also surrounded by history. You have only to lift your eyes to see the heights of towering Mount Nebo from which Moses viewed the promised land. You may also see through the air, whose odd quality makes distances uncertain and confusing, the sacred eminence known as the Mount of Temptation.

To your left in the mountains overlooking the sea are the ruins of Machaerus, the palace or fortress where Salome danced before Herod and won as a reward the bleeding head of John the Baptist on a charger. From this spot you may look across the wilderness of Judea in which the doughty prophet so sternly declaimed. To your right is discernible the area of Khirbet Qumran, scene of the dramatic modern discovery of the Dead Sea Scrolls. Finally as you gaze from north to south and east to west you behold the mountains of Moab, of Gilead and Judea under which stirring panorama much of the great religious history and heritage of mankind was developed. Jesus, of course, knew every mile of this territory and that which we now look upon He often saw. And over all this terrain through which we travel, He also passed on His deeds of love and mercy. Here He preached and taught. Truly we are now literally walking where Jesus walked.

8

The Romance of Qumran

M Y FAMILY AND I MADE AN UNFORGETTABLE EXCURSION TO Khirbet Qumran with Yusef Saad, distinguished Curator of the Palestine Archaeological Museum of Jerusalem, Jordan. Skirting the Dead Sea we left the highway and jounced over a rough track on the desert for some five miles. Dr. Saad gunned the car up a steep slope, and brought it to a dust-swirling stop. We had arrived at the recently excavated ruins of the ancient Essene village of Khirbet Qumran. The community was founded about 125 B.C., and here the famous Dead Sea Scrolls were written from that time until A.D. 65. In a mountain cave nearby they were accidentally found by a Bedouin shepherd in 1947.

The story begins many years before the birth of Christ. The world was in chaos even then, as it is at present with wars and rumors of wars. Powerful nations such as Egypt, Assyria, Persia and Rome kept the ancient world in an uproar. Under the influence of Alexander the Great, men everywhere began to be dominated by Greek ways and Greek thought, which also invaded Jewish life and religion.

A group of deeply spiritual men called the Essenes left Jerusalem in protest against what they considered a profaning of their faith, and withdrew into the desert to await the end of the world. The Essenes, according to Josephus and Philo, were an ascetic sect who maintained a severe and Spartan spiritual life. Punishment for infractions of the communities' rules was stringent. For speaking unkindly so as to undermine the composure of a fellow, the offender's food ration was reduced for one year. For falling asleep or spitting during a session of the group, the food ration was reduced for thirty days.

The Essenes' guiding principles were ritualistic purity and apocalypticism (expectation of a near ending of the world). Like the first Christians they held everything in common and looked forward to a new age ruled by unity, brotherhood and love. They identified themselves with the "Congregation of the Poor" and with the "meek" who shall "inherit the earth."

Study of the religious law was so vital to the Essenes that they worked in three shifts around the clock, studying and meditating upon Scripture and copying manuscripts. These were later stored for safekeeping in nearby caves. The sect was under the direction of twelve elders and three priests "perfect in all that is revealed of the law to practice truth and righteousness and justice and loving devotion and to walk humbly each with his neighbor to guard faithfulness with a strong purpose and a broken spirit."

Their village at Khirbet Qumran is remarkably preserved and indicates a highly self-sufficient community. There is a well-engineered conduit for supplying rain water conserved in the Wadi Qumram for winter rains. The water was then kept in deep cisterns. Nearby is a farm where foodstuffs were raised for the ancient community. The settlement shows some of the characteristics of a medieval monastery, for it has a sturdy lookout-tower constructed of walls three feet thick. There are refectories, kitchen, scriptorium (writing room) for manuscript work, flour mills, storage bins, ovens and a pottery-making center. The excavators found stacked against the wall of one room more than a thousand bowls, dishes, plates and jugs, suggesting a large pantry.

Dr. Saad has on exhibit in the Palestine Archaeological Museum in Jerusalem (one of the best equipped museums in the eastern world), a fine collection of pottery from the excavations. Some of the jars are intact, or nearly so, after two thousand years.

One of the most interesting objects found in the excavations was a tumbled mass of white plaster on mud bricks. When sorted out and put together, the pieces became a long high bench with a lower bench behind it. Archaeologists believe these were tables used by scribes in copying manuscripts. This theory is supported by two inkpots containing dried ink found in the same debris. This, incidentally, is a carbon ink said to be the most lasting that can be made. The tables may have fallen from an upper story when the building was destroyed.

As we stand in the center of this Essene village we can with little effort reconstruct imaginatively the happenings of those far-off days in A.D. 68 which have come to light in our time to electrify modern man. This is another of those incidents in Holy Land history in which we can almost hear the voices of men centuries dead and enter with them into the stirring

In these famous caves behind the Essene village on the Dead Sea shore, the manuscripts known as the Dead Sea Scrolls were hidden from the world from A.D. 68 to A.D. 1947.

events of their lives. It is as though they had only just gone away for a while after hiding their precious documents for safekeeping. But they never returned and the slow centuries almost forgot them until a Bedouin shepherd 2,000 years later shied a stone into a cave high on the mountainside and heard the crash of pottery.

The story of the discovery and later history of the Scrolls is told in various versions, but it seems that the boy climbed into the cave hoping to find hidden treasure. Instead he found jars containing only some old hardened rolls of leather, though not all manuscripts were in jars. It was decided to try to sell them to an antiquities dealer. Several turned them down as worthless. After some months a sale was made to a monastery in Jerusalem where they were thought to be very ancient. Just how valuable they were was ultimately realized, and in time high prices were paid for the Scrolls or parts thereof. The Dead Sea Scrolls, as these were to be called, are considered among the great discoveries of modern times; priceless Biblical manuscripts over two thousand years old.

Almost six hundred manuscripts have been found in eleven caves in the Qumran area, and others of later date have been found south and west of

Qumran. About one third of the manuscripts are books of the Old Testament, excluding Esther. The manuscripts contain hymns, liturgies, wisdom books and documents relating to the regulations of the Essene sect. Most are in Hebrew, but there are others in Aramaic and a few in Greek. They are chiefly written on leather, some are on papyrus, and one is on copper.

We may imaginatively identify with events of the past as we walk about the Essenes' village and look up at those lonely caves in the mountainside. In the meeting room of the community that fateful day in A.D. 68 the elders excitedly took counsel. A crisis was at hand. Roman legionnaries were clanking down the road from Caesarea and already were at Jericho, hardly more than 6 miles to the north. Before the Romans moved on Jerusalem they would surely fall upon their village. The sacred scrolls must be saved from these vandals of paganism.

These are the excavated ruins of the Essene village, which stood on an eminence overlooking the Dead Sea. Here were copied the manuscripts of the Scriptures, which at the approach of the Romans in A.D. 68 were hastily stored for safe-keeping in nearby mountain caves and were not to be discovered for nineteen centuries.

Quickly the precious documents were gathered together and a few carefully placed in large earthen jars, each tightly closed, the top being firmly held in place by a sturdy leather thong. Other manuscripts were picked up hastily as they were, and all were then carried by the younger and more agile brothers (one must be agile to make the ascent) to caves high up on a precipice. There the jars and manuscripts were carefully stored far back in the dark recesses. Feeling that their pious and sacred works were now safely hidden from the enemy, the brothers went away fully expecting to return when safety was assured.

The Romans came as feared. A number must have stayed for an extended time, for some remains of soldiers, women and children have been found in the nearby Essene cemetery (a large one with nearly 1,000 graves). There is some evidence that the community came to a violent end. The brothers apparently never returned—though, may it not be possible that one or two of the more daring came back disguised as sons of the desert to make certain of the safety of their precious jars?

Time closed in and for nearly 20 centuries the Essene brothers were practically forgotten, save for a dim and tenuous tradition concerning them which persevered. The long centuries passed during which great Rome fell. The conquering armies of the Arabs marched nearby and for many centuries ruled the entire region from beyond the Tigris and Euphrates to the Mediterranean. The crusaders came and went. Christianity grew to be a world region. The Turks came and governed for 400 years before the British mandate.

And no one at any time suspected the great secret hidden in the caves above Qumran, for the community center had sunk beneath the drifting sands of the desert. Then one day the Bedouin shepherd shied a stone into a mountain cave, and so it was that after 20 centuries Qumran burst into the life of the modern world.

Sunset on the Mediterranean at Caesara, Israel.

9

By the Walls of Jericho

A GREAT HOST WAS GATHERED OVER JORDAN. WE LOOK ACROSS THE famous river, and by exercising a little imagination we can almost make it out. In the illusory light it is almost a historical mirage on the far-reaching desert land. The place where we now stand is at least very near to where the children of Israel under Joshua crossed over the Jordan and camped in the land of Gilgal.

Joshua had sent to Jericho two spies who got a room in the house (Dr. Frank Slaughter calls it an inn) of a harlot named Rahab. She was a smart girl, for she knew all about this big army poised only a few miles away and realized that Jericho could not hold out for long. Wanting to save her own pretty skin she made a deal with the spies. In return for hiding them, she and her family were to be saved, even if everyone else in town was slaughtered. It was also agreed that a scarlet cord (a very appropriate color) should hang from her window to identify her residence. Her house was built into the wall, and therefore the scarlet cord would be clearly evident to the attackers.

The king of Jericho heard that the spies were in town and, knowing Rahab's shady reputation, figured they might have made for her place. He sent soldiers to make a search, but she sweetly beguiled them, so to speak—and doubtless she knew from experience how to do just that. She had hidden the spies under some stalks of flax on her roof, and so got away with her traitorous act of self-preservation. Later she let them down over the walls and they made their escape.

65

The Temple of Jupiter at Baalbek.

What an amazing sight it must have been here at this Jordan crossing on that far-off day when the Ark of the Covenant was carried over the stream. The people were supposed to come no nearer to the venerated object than 2,000 cubits (3,000 feet). Joshua made a speech telling his followers that the owners of the land across the Jordan, namely, the Canaanites, the Hittites, the Perizzites, the Girgashites, the Amorites and the Jebusites would all be driven from their farms and homes and nations, and the children of Israel would take over. He assured them that God would help them do this.

Joshua also told his people that when the feet of the priests bearing the Ark should rest in the Jordan, the water would "stand up in a heap" so that the priests in the middle of the river would walk on absolutely dry land. Indeed, all the people would pass over the river on dry land.

This phenomenon may have a natural cause to which the wily Old Testament writer gave a supernatural connotation. The stoppage of the stream was said to be many miles above at "the city Adam, that is beside Zaretan." (Joshua 3:16) Actually, the flow of the Jordan River has been blocked a number of times in recorded history, most recently in 1927 when the fall of a high cliff dammed the stream for 21 hours. This normal act of nature took place in the very area mentioned in the Bible.

The Bible goes on to tell us that after the people, to the number of about 40,000, passed over a dry Jordan river bed they encamped in the land of Gilgal. This is the very country through which we ourselves passed to get to the Jordan River.

The citizens of doomed Jericho got ready for battle. The gates were closed, the walls manned. No one was allowed to pass in or out of the city. Joshua impressed upon his people that the Lord personally was telling him just what to do at each step. His men of war were to encompass the city and march entirely round it once every day for six days. Seven priests were to carry before the Ark seven trumpets of rams' horns. Then the priests were to give a big blast on the rams' horns, at which point all the people were to shout as loudly as possible, and the walls of the city would immediately fall down flat. And that, so we are told, is exactly what happened.

The distinguished British archaeologist, Kathleen Kenyon, whose important work on the site of this ancient city is described in her book, *Digging Up Jericho*, has the following to say:

> But as to what caused the walls to fall down flat we have no factual evidence. We can guess that it was an earthquake, which the excava-

tions have shown to have destroyed a number of the earlier walls, but this is only conjecture. It would have been very natural for the Israelites to have regarded such a visitation as divine intervention on their behalf, as indeed it can be regarded.

Miss Kenyon, incidentally, tends to date this destruction of Jericho in the latest Bronze Age, around the third quarter of the Fourteenth Century B.C.

At any rate, Joshua reminded his men to be sure to take good care of their friend, the harlot Rahab, but to get busy and kill everyone else. They carried out their leader's command to the letter, killing with the sword every man, woman, little child, everybody young and old in the town, even animals. When they got through with their bloody work, at the site of this big mound, or tell, where we now stand, no one was alive in Jericho except the canny harlot Rahab and her family, all no doubt illegitimate. Then they burned the city, but, naturally, they first took all the gold and silver they could find.

But this wasn't all. Standing on the smoldering ruins of Jericho, that once fine, walled town, with the bloody bodies of the murdered piled high around him, Joshua, the Lord's chosen servant, spat out these words: "Cursed be the man before the Lord that riseth up and buildeth this city Jericho." (Joshua 6:26) To say the least, he didn't sound too Godly and loving. Commenting on Joshua's curse, Miss Kenyon says: "The first man in the Bible who defied the curse, and paid the penalty in the loss of his first born and youngest son was Hiel the Bethelite in the time of Ahab, that is to say about 880 B.C. On this evidence there would be a gap in occupation of some 450 years."

It would seem that the harsh God described here varies rather considerably from the loving Heavenly Father in Whom we are taught to believe; from that creative God of love upon Whom a world of brotherhood might be developed. These good people must have conveniently forgotten those presumably important tablets Moses found on Sinai, especially the one that said, "Thou shalt not kill."

But in this connection I was impressed by the statement of one of our greatest Holy Land archaeologists, W. F. Albright, who said, "The Bible never hides the wickedness of men. . . . There is a little bit of Belsen, Dachau, Auschwitz in all of us. There but for the Grace of God would I be."

It helps in our understanding to hold the thought that out of evil, good may come, that in and through it all God had an unfolding purpose. Out of superstition comes enlightenment; out of cruelty, love. Strange, perhaps,

From a shoulder of the Mount of Temptation can be seen one of the largest refugee camps in the world. Here live some 80,000 Arabs who fled penniless from their homes in the border war of 1948. The first temporary housing has given way to a clean city of refuge.

but it can be so. We can only hope and pray that over the long centuries man may improve.

After one of our visits here in the Jordan valley, we went at twilight to a friend's cottage located on a shoulder of the Mount of Temptation, that grim and historic height that broods over the Jericho plain. It was the Fourth of July, and a few of us, Americans far from home, gathered for a picnic. I found it hard to accept the incongruity: think of it, a picnic on the Mount of Temptation! It was certainly no picnic for Jesus Who, higher up on this same mountain, fought the lonely battle of temptation. In this wilderness He fasted for 40 days and nights. And the mountain was a place of temptation for Him. Here He repulsed Satan who "sheweth Him all the kingdoms of the world, and the glory of them; And saith unto Him, All these things will I give Thee, if Thou wilt fall down and worship me." (Matt. 4:8-9)

On that memorable Fourth of July we watched spellbound as twilight came to the vast plain, coloring the mountains of Judea and Moab and Gilead. The sun dropped, a flaming red ball, into the Dead Sea and long shadows fell over this beloved land where once walked the great prophets of our religious heritage; where our kindly and loving Saviour struggled in temptation so that He might teach us how to live.

Then night came and the lights of Jericho twinkled in the darkness. Modern Jericho is some two miles from its ancient site. Nearby, spreading over a large area on the plain, is one of the largest refugee camps in the world housing nearly 80,000 persons who fled penniless during the Arab-Israeli war in 1948. The temporary housing has given way to a seemingly permanent city of refuge, and many of these unfortunate people are finding new opportunity for themselves in the growing economy of Jordan.

Joshua's curse upon Jericho seemed to have worked. As stated earlier, it lay in ruins for several centuries. But subsequently, because of the exotic vegetation which can grow there, a new city grew up. In fact, Mark Antony once gave the city and region to his friend Cleopatra, who seemed to like the balsam gardens of Jericho very much indeed. She had wanted to be Queen of Judea, but Antony talked her out of it, and she fell quite in love with Jericho. And that is not to be wondered at, for it's a lovely place of perfumes, sweet-scented oils and other aromatic products, all of which might well have attracted this lady. Besides, it produced revenue. H. V. Morton points out that the richness of Jericho can be estimated from the fact that Cleopatra rented her balsam groves to Herod for a yearly sum of two hundred talents, the equivalent of approximately $150,000.

Herod, apparently desiring to get the full worth of his money, built a Roman town of his own some two miles from modern Jericho. In this era Jericho reached its peak of importance and prosperity. It contained a splendid amphitheater, hippodrome and other usual structures, the most sumptuous of which was his own winter palace, which was surrounded by lush gardens. One can walk over the palace ruins, which have been excavated, and remember that in this salubrious place, where only balmy breezes blow in winter, disease-riddled Herod breathed his last in 4 B.C. after a life of sin and cruelty.

Returning once again to the tell, or mound, of ancient Canaanite Jericho, the one destroyed by Joshua, we see Elisha's spring, the waters of which the prophet sweetened by casting into the fountain a handful of salt. I feel sure you will hold ever in memory the vision of women from the refugee village coming to Elisha's spring and carrying away water jars on their heads (or in many cases large discarded oil cans). The grace and charm of these women is one of the memories of Jericho.

The winding Jericho road, the one which figured in the immortal story of the Good Samaritan, is now a wide, well-engineered modern highway. This area, arid in summer, is carpeted with wild flowers in the spring.

10

New Life
in the Wilderness of Judea

WE GO NOW TO THE BANKS OF THE JORDAN TO ANOTHER VERY famous and sacred spot, the scene of the baptism of our Lord Jesus Christ by John the Baptist.

On the way we stop in the shade under the spreading branches of a huge, old sycamore tree. Whether this is the actual place where Zacchaeus climbed into the branches to see Jesus pass by is not important. One thing is sure—it couldn't have been very far from this spot that a wonderful demonstration of the way Jesus worked with people was given to every Zacchaeus who wistfully wants a better life.

Crowds lined the streets of Jericho that day, for word had gotten about that the beloved Teacher and Healer was coming through. In the throng was a rich man of Jericho, a publican, perhaps chief customs officer of the whole district, named Zacchaeus.

He was a forthright and dauntless sort of character and, though short of stature, was determined to get a good look at the great Prophet. He tried bobbing between the shoulders of taller people, but he just couldn't see well enough, so he solved the problem by climbing a sycamore tree. As He came along, Jesus saw this man perched in the branches. With his keen insight, He understood this man and almost surprised him into falling from the tree when He said, "Zacchaeus, make haste, and come down, for today I must abide at thy house." (Luke 19:5)

Of course the falsely pious grumbled that the Lord should select a money grabber as His host. Jesus knew precisely what He was doing. He realized that this man had much more in him than showed on the surface. And sure enough, it wasn't long before the little rich man resolved to

straighten out his dealings, and actually promised to give half of his hold-
ings to the poor.

So Zacchaeus climbed more than a tree when he saw Jesus that day.
Indeed, he climbed high up into a new life. This story is an illustration of
the amazing manner in which the Master stimulates and motivates men
toward being their better selves. Could be this is one reason we ourselves
are here at Jericho trying to see Jesus.

It was in such an ancient sycamore tree that the tax collector,
Zacchaeus, climbed to see over the heads of the throng as Jesus
passed by.

Along the way we pause for a brief visit at the Umayyad Palace at
Khirbet al-Mafjar. It was built in all probability for the Caliph Hisham
ibn Abdul Malik, who ruled the vast Arab dominions from 724 to 743.
Like most Arab rulers he preferred the freedom and space of desert living.
The remarkable excavations of the palace, revealing splendid mosaics and
stucco ornaments, are excellent examples of Umayyad art and architecture.
This palace was built, of course, long after the time of Christ's earthly
ministry, but it unmistakably conveys one interesting aspect of this area's
flavor.

It was in this wide territory through which we have been traveling, the
wilderness of Judea, that one of the most picturesque and strongest individuals of history stirred up the natives. This man, John the Baptist, must

easily rank with the greatest orators of all time, and people came for miles to hear him. St. Matthew tells about it, "Then went out to him Jerusalem, and all Judea, and all the region round about Jordan, And were baptized of him in Jordan, confessing their sins." (Matt. 3:5-6)

Some of us preachers who can't draw people from across the street might well study this preacher who pulled them for miles across mountains and desert. Moreover, members of his congregation had no motor cars, but came on donkeyback or afoot over rough, rocky roads. Nor did they have an air-conditioned, soft-seated auditorium in which to listen to his sermons. They sat in the boiling sun and liked it.

Don't imagine he was short-winded, either. He must have been such a speaker as no longer exists in this soft world of nice little essay sermons by "scholarly" men clad in Madison Avenue styles. John the Baptist was no glamour boy—far from it. He was a browned, hairy giant who probably never had a haircut. Nor was he much of a dresser. In fact, he wore only a rough garment of camel's hair tied around his lean middle with a strong leather girdle. I say "lean middle," for how could it be otherwise, since he ate only locusts and what honey he could find. Calories were no problem to him. He must have been not only lean, but also tough and hard as nails.

The immense drawing power of this colorful person was surprising, because when we read what few fragments we have of his sermons, they are counter to all the rules for popularity. He really talked tough. He feared neither man nor the devil, nor the king; and fearlessness of the king was what finished him. He looked out over his huge congregation and spied some religious big shots, the Pharisees and Sadducees; and I'm sure you never heard any preacher address anyone in a congregation as did John. Raising his gravelly, booming voice, and pointing directly at them, he said, "O generation of vipers . . ." (Matt. 3:7), that is to say, "You mess of snakes." Pretty strong? And how! But perhaps that could be just one thing that drew people; the fact that he was not afraid of anyone.

He had conviction and what we today call guts, and that evokes grudging admiration, even if some toes are stepped on. But it wasn't only the religious leaders that he castigated, which presumably might have made him popular with the crowd. St. Luke points out that he included everybody in that "generation of vipers" designation.

He pointed out that it would do them no good to fall back upon a religious heritage to save them from the wrath to come, but they had to repent and live better lives, for "every tree which bringeth not forth good fruit is hewn down, and cast into the fire." (Matt. 3:10) Of course, if you are concerned about saving your own skin, such forthright talk is dangerous, especially as specific as John made it when he publicly attacked Herod's lack of morality for unlawfully taking Herodias, the wife of his brother Philip.

This woman hated John for these potent remarks, and wanted to have him killed, but Herod was afraid to touch John, regarding him as a holy man. However, as you know, she tricked the king into promising her daughter Salome anything she wanted "unto the half of my kingdom" (Mark 6:23), because she pleased him by her sensual dancing. When Salome asked for the head of John the Baptist, he couldn't renege, for there were many witnesses to his promise. If John had winked at this sinfulness in high places, as some who don't want to stir up anything, he would not have lost his head. But then, in that event, he might have lost his soul, and when you have to choose between soul and head, what can you do?

John baptized great crowds in the river Jordan, telling them thereafter to live Godly lives. Many people were so impressed by John that they began to say he was the long-awaited Christ, or Messiah. But he humbly said another would come so much greater than he that he wasn't even worthy to put the water upon His head. But Jesus insisted, and when it was done, "he saw the Spirit of God descending like a dove, and lighting upon Him: And lo a voice from heaven, saying, This is my beloved Son, in whom I am well pleased." (Matt. 3:16-17)

One looks at this sylvan spot, the softly flowing river with green-covered banks, and reflects that it must appear now much as then. I baptized several young men here one day, and asked one of them to put Jordan water on my head in an act of rededication.

At this spot on the River Jordan, Jesus was baptized by John the Baptist.

There is just one more stop I want you to make before we go up to Jerusalem. We retrace our steps through the land of Gilgal and through the wilderness of Judea where John the Baptist preached.

I shall take you to the big green ranch of a friend of mine here in the Jordan valley. You are going to see what can happen to a wilderness when a positive thinker goes to work on it. His name is Musa Alami and he has made the desert blossom as the rose. He succeeded because he believed that he could, and he kept at it until he did.

Musa, an Arab boy, was educated at Cambridge and then returned to Palestine where he became a well-to-do man—well-to-do, that is, by Middle Eastern standards. Then in the political turmoil he lost everything, including his home.

A Jordanian shepherd plays his flute while the sheep graze on the rocky soil. This spot is by the ancient road from Jerusalem to Damascus over which Saul of Tarsus passed on his mission of persecuting the Christians.

He went beyond Jordan to the edge of Jericho. Stretching away on either side was the great, bleak, arid desert of the Jordan valley. In the distance to the left loomed the mountains of Judea, and to the right, the mountains of Moab.

With the exception of a few oases, nothing had ever been cultivated in this hot and weary land and all the wiseacres said that nothing could be raised, for how could you bring water to it? To dam the Jordan River for irrigation was too expensive, and besides there was no friendly power to finance such a project.

"What about underground water?" asked Musa Alami. Long and loud they laughed. Who ever heard of such a thing? There was no water under that hot, dry desert. That sandy waste of parched earth and sand had lain there since the beginning of time. And having been covered ages ago by Dead Sea water, the sand was full of salt, which further added to its aridity.

Musa, meditating, saw the shimmering surface of the Dead Sea nearby and agreed that the saltiness of the earth was indeed a problem. But weren't problems put in our way only to be solved? God, he reasoned, had made it a good earth and all that was necessary was to bring life-giving water to it.

He had heard of the amazing rehabilitation of the California desert through subsurface water. He decided that he could find water here also. So sure was he that he mapped out roads for a ranch. All the old-time Bedouin sheiks said it couldn't be done; famous scientists from abroad agreed. There was absolutely no water there. That was that.

But Musa was unimpressed. A few poverty-stricken refugees from the nearby Jericho Refugee Camp helped him as he started to dig, with only pick and shovel. Everybody laughed as the dauntless man and his ragged friends dug away day after day, week after week, month after month.

For six mouths they dug. Then one day the sand became wet, and finally water, life-giving water, gushed forth. The Arabs who had gathered round did not laugh or cheer; they wept. Water had been found in the ancient desert! And they who had known the burning sands for centuries could not speak, so great was their wonder and gratitude.

Now, several years later, Musa Alami has fifteen wells supplying a ranch nearly three miles long and two miles wide. He raises vegetables, bananas, figs, citrus fruit and boys. In his school he is growing citizens of the future,

Boys left homeless by the Arab-Israeli conflict are being trained at a wonderful "Boys' Town" school conducted by Musa Alami on his exotic ranch near Jericho. Here, our friend and tour leader, John Huffman, and Mrs. Cecelia Ketchum talk with some of these bright and attractive boys. They are taught to a high degree of skill in trades and advanced desert agriculture.

farmers and technicians, experts in the trades. Produce is flown to Kuwait, Bahrein, the Persian Gulf, Beirut, as well as to nearby Jerusalem. Imitating Musa, others have also dug until forty thousand acres are under cultivation and the green is spreading over the sands.

I asked this amazing man what kept him going, kept him believing when everyone said it couldn't be done. "There was no alternative. It had to be done," he said; and added, "God helped me."

11

Up to Jerusalem

NOW WE GO UP TO JERUSALEM AND UP INDEED IT IS. BEGINNING AT Jericho we shall rise from approximately 1,300 feet below sea level to 2,800 feet above sea level (15 miles as the crow flies, nearly 25 miles as the road twists), or approximately 4,000 feet in about forty minutes.

As we move speedily by car over a magnificent highway up to the Holy City, remember that our Lord, Who often made this trip, walked the climb over a rough road, a large section of which still remains. I once took this old Roman road going down to Jericho. It is composed of huge, chariot-rutted paving blocks and the grade is steep and hard. Perhaps now and then Jesus made the trip on the back of a little donkey, such as you often see in this land; but mostly He walked.

About halfway up from Jericho to Jerusalem, we come to the Inn of the Good Samaritan, called Khan Hathrur by the Arabs. It is a modern structure used as a Jordanian police station. Uniformed soldiers wearing colorful red and white kufiyehs (headpieces) are always on guard. The present building stands on the site of a very ancient inn. Excellent examples of ancient walls and mosaics are visible, and exceedingly old rock cisterns on the site indicate that a building has been here since Bible times. Even now, despite modern progress, this is practically the only building on the route between Bethany and the outskirts of Jericho.

The Jericho road was notorious from earliest days for brigandism. This was so because of its loneliness and isolation and infinite numbers of hiding places in the mountainous, desert country through which the road

This highway rises from 1,200 feet below to 2,500 feet above sea level within 25 miles from Jericho to Jerusalem.

passes. H. V. Morton in his delightful book, *In the Steps of the Master*, tells how he was warned as recently as 30 years ago not to travel this road after dark lest he be held up by a bandit having the picturesque name of Abu Jildah. This bandit had gathered considerable local fame and prowess in building walls of stone across the road, thus halting cars and permitting him to relieve travelers of their possessions. Once, Morton relates, Abu had as many as 14 cars lined up, and he and his band robbed all aboard. Also, he was not too averse to shooting anyone who refused to cooperate. But this state of affairs no longer exists because of the firm administration of the nation. I have been up and down this road many times, day and night, and have always found it safe.

The Inn of the Good Samaritan was immortalized in one of the wonderful stories used by Jesus, the Master Teacher, to make clear His way of

Here is the traditional site of the Inn of the Good Samaritan on the road between Jerusalem and Jericho.

life. It came from a question put to Him by a not too friendly person who hoped to trap Jesus into a denial of the Jewish concept of brotherhood. The question was "Who is my neighbor?" The sly questioner supposed Jesus would have to conform to the strict interpretation that a Jew can only be brother or neighbor to another Jew.

But with His marvelous ability to make great truths simple and crystal clear, Jesus lifted the concept of brotherhood to new levels by telling a story that has endured through the ages. Inasmuch as the Master was traveling this very territory at the time, it is quite likely that His story was inspired by an actual happening along this way.

At any rate He told about a man who went down from Jerusalem to Jericho. He fell among thieves who cleaned him of all he had, even stripped him of his clothing. They beat him unmercifully, leaving the poor fellow lying along the road bleeding and half-dead. Presently a priest came along and heard the victim groaning in his pain. The beat-up fellow looked pretty messy to this dilettante priest. He didn't want to soil his soft hands; anyway he figured someone else would come along and take care of the battered-up unfortunate. So he passed him up. True, someone else did come along, but he also was a false religious leader, in this case, a Levite. He was no doubt on some "profound" business for the hierarchy and therefore dealing with such important matters as to have no time for one wounded man. He, too, after looking the victim over from a distance, passed on.

Not so the next man who came by. He was not a religious official, nor was he a Jew. Actually he was a Samaritan, lowest of the low, one of a race of people for whom religious Jews had no use at all. But the Samaritan proved that he had a good heart. He at once got down from his donkey and cleansed the traveler's wounds by pouring on them oil and wine for disinfectant purposes. Then he heaved the groggy fellow onto his donkey and brought him to this inn. He stayed overnight to take care of the stranger, and in the morning, when he had to go on, left money with the hotel keeper to pay for the man's care—even promising to pay any additional expense on his way back. When Jesus asked which of the three was the real neighbor, what other possible answer was there? The real neighbor was "He that shewed mercy." (Luke 10:37)

Seeing another's needs and supplying them without question of racial or religious status is indeed obedience to Jesus' teachings. Maybe we could very well use a new emphasis on this important truth. So, fellow pilgrim to the Holy Land, I suggest sending our cars on ahead for perhaps a half-mile and walking this road on foot for a little way. And as we walk, let us ask ourselves whether we have true Christian neighborly love in our own

80   UP TO JERUSALEM

hearts and whether we show mercy along life's road to those of other races and faiths. We might each of us raise the question whether our love is limited only to those nearest us and to those who belong to our own groups? Such soul searching is an intrinsic feature of our visit to the land where Jesus first taught the truths by which we Christians promise to live. One thing is sure: the parable of the Good Samaritan will live with you forever once you have personally identified with it.

Soon now, around a bend in the road ahead, we shall see for the first time Jerusalem the Golden, gleaming on its hills. The tall church tower on the Mount of Olives can be seen at intervals from miles away as the road twists and turns, winding its way up through the mountains of Judea.

On our way up to the Holy City we soon come to the village of el-Azariyeh, the site of the ancient village of Bethany. It lies on a shoulder of the Mount of Olives scarcely two miles from Jerusalem. Although new houses and commercial buildings are being erected along the busy highway, as soon as you enter the village itself the flavor of Biblical times is clearly evident. It looks as if it came straight out of the Bible—just like scenes in the Bible picture books we read as children.

Jesus loved Bethany and often came here to rest at the home of his friends, Lazarus, Mary and Martha. The ruins of the house of Lazarus and his sisters are pointed out to us on our visit and we are shown also the remains of the house of Simon the Leper. It was in this house that Jesus sat at dinner when a woman came with an alabaster box of precious ointment

This is the tomb of Lazarus at Bethany, through the door of which the dead man appeared at Jesus' command, "Lazarus, come forth." (John 11:43)

The great Roman theatre at Amman, capital of Jordan, is shown here. The photograph shows graphically the attractive modern city with this monumental reminder of antiquity at its center. More than six thousand persons may be seated in the mounting tiers.

and anointed Him. Jesus was so touched by this act of kindness and sacrifice that He said, "Wheresoever this gospel shall be preached in the whole world, there shall also this, that this woman hath done, be told for a memorial of her." (Matt. 26:13)

Once here in this little village I had one of the great spiritual moments of my life. The background of this experience occurred many years ago when I was a boy and with my family stood by an open grave in southern Ohio. The body of my grandmother was being committed to the ground. The old-fashioned country preacher standing by the grave was white of hair, kindly of face and dressed in a Prince Albert coat of the type worn by preachers in those days. Framed by a background of Ohio hills, he repeated with deep feeling those great words first spoken in Bethany: "I am the resurrection, and the life: he that believeth in me, though he were dead, yet shall he live: And whosoever liveth and believeth in me shall never die." (John 11:25-26)

As the preacher spoke these words a flash of light seemed to penetrate my mind and a warm feeling came into my heart. Boy though I was, I knew, without a doubt, that these words were true. Faith unshakable took hold of me that day.

Many years later I came to Bethany and stood with my wife and children in the brilliant sunshine just outside the dark entrance to the Tomb

View of Bethlehem from the Church of the Nativity bell tower.

of Lazarus. I wanted to hear the words again, and at the very place where they were first spoken. My wife opened the Bible and read from the Gospel of St. John the lovely story of the death and raising of Lazarus. This particular moment I shall remember as long as life shall last: my wife reading from the Old Book; the youthful, serious faces of my three children, and the dusty road where Jesus actually stood. The meaningful words which He spoke long ago fell softly in the beloved accents of my wife's voice: "I am the resurrection, and the life . . ."

Suddenly the same perception of the truth of the text which I had experienced as a boy warmed my heart. I knew once again that those who die in the Lord do not die but live forever. That day we talked of all the millions of believers who have been comforted, as they laid their dead away, by the great things Jesus said in Bethany nearly twenty centuries ago. We had come to our spiritual home; we had found once again the assurance of immortality.

12

Walking
the Palm Sunday Road

WE LEAVE OUR CAR AT BETHANY AND TAKE A NARROW, STONY road up to the Mount of Olives. This most likely is the path over which Jesus and His disciples passed between Bethany and Jerusalem. It is a rather hard walk. But I find that I like doing the hard thing here. Perhaps in so doing I can share just a slight bit more with Jesus Who surely walked such a path.

As we climb upward, vistas of Jerusalem appear through the olive trees. We trudge in silence, but it is a deep, moving silence as we try to feel worthy of walking these sacred miles. The path is steep and narrow and dusty. At last we come to the place known for centuries as Dominus Flevit, in memory of the weeping of our Lord over Jerusalem. We ask ourselves if perhaps He weeps over us and our city and our world.

We continue to the Church of the Pater Noster originally built to mark the place where Jesus talked to His disciples about the coming end of the age, and also where He taught them The Lord's Prayer. The prayer, written in many languages, adorns the walls of the colonnade of the church.

Along the way we enter a small dome-shaped chapel dating to crusader times. It was erected on the site of a much older chapel destroyed by the Persians in A.D. 614. This is presumed to be the spot from which Jesus ascended into Heaven. A stone under an opening in the floor is marked as the place the Saviour's feet last touched on earth.

We also visit Bethpage, the little village where the disciples took the ass, and a colt with her, upon which Christ rode in triumphal entry into Jerusalem. Every year on Palm Sunday the Franciscan Fathers lead a pro-

83

The Church of the Pater Noster was erected on the spot where Jesus taught the Lord's Prayer to His disciples. The prayer in many languages is on the walls of the cloister.

cession from this village to the Church of St. Anne in Jerusalem, thus retracing as nearly as possible the route taken on that first Palm Sunday so long ago.

As we reach the heights of the Mount of Olives a marvelous view eastward holds us entranced. At twilight when the heat-haze of the day has lifted we see in the far distance the Dead Sea and the Jordan valley. A long, weaving line of green marks the course of the river Jordan, and the great blue sea lies clearly defined in shafts of sunlight. The mountains of Moab and Gilead are swept by colorful light as the lengthening shadows of coming evening seek to dispute the effulgence of the setting sun. From this vantage point, with its wide panorama of Jerusalem, the scene of much of the great action of the Gospel spreads before us. In that area took place some of the greatest events in the spiritual history of mankind.

I like to approach Jerusalem on foot at twilight. The best time for photographers is morning, when the city lies in bright clear eastern sunlight. But at twilight there is often a hazy, mystical lighting effect that is little short of ethereal. It produces an ever-changing blending of soft pastel shades that invests the entire panorama of the city and Judean hills with a glory that must be from Heaven itself. The city behind its massive walls seems to float in a golden haze. Perhaps it was at such an hour that Jesus, Who loved this glorious city but Who realized its tragedy, wept over it.

The road takes us now downhill to a beloved and sacred Garden. Lying serenely at the foot of the Mount of Olives, Gethsemane was at the time of Jesus a quiet country retreat to which the Master often retired for an evening of prayer and meditation. Here He spent those terrible hours of His agony, and here He suffered betrayal by Judas Iscariot. Here at midnight He was arrested by soldiers of the High Priest.

The Palm Sunday Road from Bethphage on the Mount of Olives passes Gethsemane and on across the Kidron into the Holy City. It is believed to be the very road over which Jesus passed amidst palm-waving crowds.

The Garden today is small in area, perhaps only a half-acre. It contains eight ancient and gnarled olive trees. These may very well be from shoots of trees under which Jesus found comfort. Some authorities think the Garden of Gethsemane originally covered a larger area of the hillside. The meaning of the name Gethsemane is "olive press," which would seem to presuppose more than eight trees. There are a few olive trees adjoining the Protestant Center near the top of the hill and these too are obviously very old. Those within the present Garden are carefully tended by the Fathers of the Franciscan Church, as if they were delicate antiques, as indeed they are.

If we could continue the Palm Sunday route that Jesus followed through the palm-waving throngs we would now cross the Kidron valley and enter the city through the Golden Gate. But that gate is closed, awaiting the Lord's return. We will, therefore, rejoin our car and proceed to the delightful and charming American Colony Hotel, hostelry extraordinary, where our dear friends, the Vester family, are our hosts. We are at last in Old Jerusalem, spiritual homeland of our souls.

On one of my visits to the Holy Land I spent an evening with some friends, American and British, in Beirut. Sitting together on a terrace overlooking the sea we watched the moon come up over the Mediterranean. We talked about world affairs and many other matters. Then the conversation turned on a discussion of the distinctive attractions of the great cities of the world—Rome, London, Paris and others.

"For me," one of the Englishmen remarked, "there is only one completely captivating city: Jerusalem."

The golden gate of Jerusalem is seen through the olive trees in the Garden of Gethsemane. The gate is closed pending the return of the Lord. He entered the city through this gate on Palm Sunday.

"Because of its Biblical associations?" I asked.

"In part," he answered. "Just as a city it has a strange fascination. Besides—" he hesitated and then continued, "I had one of my greatest experiences there. You see I lost, and then found myself in Jerusalem." He became silent and did not say more.

I had remembered this man as a rather restless, discontented individual despite his reserved and unemotional manner that is often characteristic of the cultured Britisher. But now I sensed a new quality in him—a grave and calm inner happiness of some kind.

He was associated with the United Nations Relief and Works Agency for Palestine Refugees in the Near East. In the course of the evening he said to me, "While you are here, I want to show you some of the trouble spots of this area."

Driving south in the days following I accompanied him to a few of the big camps where more than one million refugees have subsisted on relief, in rather deplorable conditions, for well over a decade. As we went about together we talked of many things, but I noticed that whenever I mentioned religion or even verged on it, he seemed always to change the subject, retreating behind a barrier of reticence.

Then one day at Jerusalem he took me down into some cellars under the ruins of a bombed-out section of the city. These dismal cellars served as improvised dwelling places for numerous refugee families who had no other place to live. As many as ten people often shared a single crowded room.

As he moved among these destitute people my friend had a helpful word or kindly gesture for each one. He greeted small children affectionately, each by name, pulling from his pocket little treats he had brought. He picked up one ragged and dirty, but very pretty, little girl, hugging her closely while he chatted with her mother. At the bedside of an old man, he sat on the coverlet, gently stroked the gray shock of hair, holding the man's frail hand for a moment in his own. These places were far from clean. But he seemed not to mind, impeccable though he was. Obviously he sincerely loved these people.

Presently we came up out of those dark cellars into the bright sunlight. There, straight ahead, clearly defined in a gap between the half-demolished walls of bombed houses, rose the Mount of Olives and on its shoulder the Garden of Gethsemane. I stood staring, deeply moved.

I became aware of my companion standing silently beside me. "You don't fool me a bit," I said when I found my voice. "The reason Jerusalem is so dear to you is that here you serve those who need help and love—and you do it in the name of the Man who suffered over there," I said, pointing to the sacred spot.

Tersely, almost gruffly, he replied, "Didn't I tell you I found myself in Jerusalem?" That was all he said, but I knew then the source of his deep happiness. He wasn't the kind to talk about it, but he had found inner contentment here.

This man had discovered a very great secret: that when we lose ourselves in loving service to others, we find ourselves, and in this finding of ourselves we also discover life's deepest happiness. Some months later he was killed in a car accident while on an errand of mercy—this man who loved Jerusalem.

The name Jerusalem was probably derived from the earliest of several names by which the city has been known from Babylonian and Egyptian literature: Urusalim, meaning "City of Salim" or "City of Peace." At a very early time it was an important stronghold controlling the desert and guarding trade routes from Hebron to Bethel and Shechem, and to Jericho and beyond. The king of Jerusalem, Melchizedek, was a ruler of great power. Indeed so strongly fortified was his city that it held out for a long time against the invading Israelites. It was finally captured by David about 1000 B.C.

The history of Jerusalem actually goes back to the Stone Age. About 2500 B.C. the country was a vassal of Egypt, as is shown by tablets found at Tell-el-Amarna, though it was actually in the hands of the Jebusites.

Jerusalem has been built and destroyed and rebuilt many times in its history. Foundations rise upon foundations, walls upon walls; and beneath the earth are other layers of buildings and walls. The accumulated rubble upon which the city has been built and rebuilt has raised the present street level at some points as much as sixty feet above the original. The streets in the Old City are on the average at least 20 feet above the level of the streets in the time of Christ.

For example, the first wall of Jerusalem may have been an ancient rampart built by the Jebusites, captured by David, repaired by him and Joab and enlarged by Solomon. About 960 B.C. Solomon built the first Temple and the wall of Jerusalem around about to protect his palaces and Temple. A great section of the "Jebusite and Solomonic" walls have been opened up and can be seen. In 790 B.C. Joash captured the city and broke down the northern wall which was later restored by Uzziah. In 586 B.C. Jerusalem was destroyed by Nebuchadnezzar and the city laid to waste, walls demolished. Then came Nehemiah about 445 B.C., and he rebuilt the walls with many gates and erected towers and other buildings.

Alexander entered Jerusalem in 332 B.C. but surprisingly his was a peaceful occupation. However, in 320 B.C. Ptolemy I of Egypt tore down the fortifications. Simon II partially restored the city in 219 B.C., only to have it go down again, Temple and all, in 168 B.C. at the hand of Antiochus Epiphanes. After this destruction the city sank to possibly its lowest ebb. Pompey took Jerusalem in 64 B.C., and Crassus plundered the Temple in 54 B.C.

Here is a view of Jerusalem, Old City, from the Mount of Olives. The Dome of the Rock and temple area are shown left of center beyond the walls.

Then Herod, a great builder-king, caused a new city, brilliant in its architcture, to rise on the many layers of ruins. Augustus, who claimed to have "found Rome brick and left it marble," held Herod in favor and both inspired and helped Herod to rebuild the Temple magnificently; erect the vast fortress Antonia; construct a superb palace, and, of course, the wall. Many of the huge foundation stones of this wall remain today. This was the city which Jesus knew and which He prophesied would be destroyed, no stone left on stone.

This destruction as foretold by Jesus occurred in A.D. 70 by Titus. The Roman Legion, which occupied Jerusalem for some 60 years after its razing by order of Caesar, left behind it thousands of indications of its presence, including small tiles placed in buildings. The tiles have the legion's number (tenth) and its emblems of a galley and a bear. The tiles are often found today in Jerusalem; indeed one was presented to me and is in my study where I write.

Following a Jewish rebellion in A.D. 132, which failed, the Jews were expelled from the Temple, the city was burned and the site plowed over. A new city was built and named Aelia Capitolina in honor of Hadrian. Temples were dedicated to Bacchus, Venus and Serapis. Over the site of Solomon's Temple, a great shrine to Jupiter Capitolinus was erected.

In about A.D. 326 Constantine, who had become a Christian, directed that the sacred site of the Crucifixion and burial be recovered and a Church of the Holy Sepulchre erected. A later church, but one also very old, stands today on the same site.

In 637 the Romans were ousted by the Arabs under Omar the Caliph, also known as Caliph Umar ibn al-Khattab, who built a wooden mosque on Mount Moriah. This is the site of the present el-Aksa Mosque, a magnificent marble structure. Caliph Abdul Malik ibn Marwan constructed the Mosque of Omar on the ancient site of the Temple of Solomon. The temple area in which it stands is called el-Haram esh-Sharif (The Noble

The Garden of Gethsemane has eight ancient olive trees, still fruit bearing, which may very well be shoots of those that stood here at the time of our Lord's agony. The adjoining structure is the Church of All Nations, or the Basilica of the Agony. Beyond is the Kidron valley, the city wall, the golden gate and the Dome of the Rock.

Sanctuary). It is built over a great rock where Abraham prepared to sacrifice his son Isaac and is known as the Dome of the Rock. It is the second (only to Mecca) holiest place in Islam and it is said that the Prophet Mohammed offered his last prayer here before ascending into Heaven.

In 1099 the crusaders, who came to recover the Cross from the infidels, entered the city and terrible carnage ensued. Apparently they were Christians with a Christian purpose, but hardly acting as Christians are presumed to act. The Moslems under Saladin retook Jerusalem in 1187 and it remained for the most part in their hands until its capture by Allenby in 1917. The present walls of the city date from the Sixteenth Century.

In 1948 Britain withdrew from Palestine and the bitter strife which exists today began. The newer part of the city lies in Israel with a wide no-man's land between it and the Old City. The old historical Holy City, surrounded by its massive medieval walls, is in Jordan as is also Bethany, Bethlehem, Gethsemane and the Mount of Olives.

13

With Jesus
in the Temple Area

THIS VOLUME IS, OF COURSE, NOT A GUIDE BOOK IN THE USUAL SENSE.
While our book is designed as an aid to the Holy Land visitor,
it is also prepared for the reader who may never actually visit
the Bible lands. My purpose in writing is to try to convey by a series of
experiences and impressions, as well as pertinent facts and descriptions,
the deep and profound meaning the Holy Land has for me. But even
more, its purpose is to bring us to a more complete identification with
the Lord Jesus Christ.

When I return to Jerusalem on successive visits, there are a few places
to which I always go and these I want to tell you about. One of the first
things I do is to go to the temple area on Mount Moriah where Solomon's
Temple stood; where later Herod the Great built the Temple that was
known the world over. That magnificent structure like a "mountain of
snow" stood in this wide esplanade in the center of which is now the
great Mosque of Omar, one of the noblest examples of Moslem architecture.

I like to sit in the shade of a column or under an arch looking across
to the Mount of Olives and Gethsemane and conjure up wonderful pictures of Jesus, scenes and incidents which happened in this place. This,
of course, is where He often came, for He loved the Temple and here,
too, is where He could have contact with people away from the thronging
bazaars in the narrow streets.

I can first see Him here as a boy of twelve, sitting in a circle of bearded
holy men and scholars, causing them to wonder at His keen perception
and His extraordinary insight.

Here, somewhere only a few feet from where we sit, an event occurred that showed another side of the meek and gentle Jesus. He had plenty of strength and sternness in His make-up and fear was no factor in His reactions. For example, one day He was teaching by the Temple when some of the Pharisees figured to scare Him away. "You had better leave here or Herod will kill you," they sneered. But did that frighten Him? Hardly. He said to them: "Go ye, and tell that fox. Behold, I cast out devils, and I do cures today and tomorrow, and the third day I shall be perfected." (Luke 13:32) He meant He was not afraid of Herod, neither he nor anybody could kill Him for more than two days.

This view of Jerusalem is from the tower of the Church of the Redeemer. This church is on the site of the crusader church of Santa Maria Latina Major, once part of the hospice of the Knights of St. John where Saladin had his head-quarters after he captured Jerusalem from the crusaders. Photograph shows the Church of the Holy Sepulchre with the two domes. This structure dates from the Twelfth Century, but is on the site of a first church built in the Fourth Century by Constantine over the presumed site of Calvary and the tomb of Christ.

This fearlessness was also demonstrated the day He walked into this temple area at the time of Passover, the holy days, and found a big traffic in oxen, sheep and doves going on. The animals were being sold for sacrifice in the Temple. The money-changers had a very lucrative racket. Money exchanged generally in business and daily affairs could not be used in connection with the Temple. It had to be changed into Temple currency and of course the money-changers, with their usual sharp tactics, were grabbing a big commission. They were swindling the people who came to worship.

The noise and shouting, the bartering and haggling, all seemed so foreign to the sacred place that Jesus could not endure it; He couldn't let it go by, the way some would as just one of those things, a so-called necessary evil. So He quickly bound some small cords together into a makeshift but effective whip. Then He went after them, the muscles standing out on His brawny arms as He lashed out left and right driving them in a docile, cringing mob out of the Temple. You can almost see them falling over one another, tumbling out of the doors, trying to get away from this bronzed giant and His whip that seemed to reach everywhere with stinging effect.

A crown of thorns was made for our photographer in Jerusalem, Jordan. It was taken from the Syrian Christ's-thorn, a bush or small tree, ten to fifteen feet high with pliant white twigs. Its stipulae have each two strong thorns which curve backward, to use Werner Keller's description. This plant grows even now in the Jerusalem area. It is believed that the crown of thorns placed on the Master's head was from this bush.

Striding through the disorganized crowd He came blazing up to the startled money-changers, the usual sly, bland type of tricksters who, like bloodsuckers, fasten themselves on decent, honest people to fleece them. With quick determined motions He up-ended their tables, money flying through the air and rolling along the paving stones. "Take these things hence; make not my Father's house a house of merchandise," he cried. (John 2:16) Did they get out? What do you think? I'll venture that a strange silence fell on this place, making it about as quiet as it is just now.

But no doubt there were many dark faces with evil looks, peering at Him from behind the safety of pillars. Weak and soft? Where did men ever pick up that ridiculous concept of the Nazarene? He was a man— a very strong man. Else that crowd would never have let Him break up their graft, that's for sure.

There are other memories of things He did in the temple area. For example, on the last and great day of the feast as the great crowds surged about Him in this huge square where the magnificent Temple once stood, Jesus must have climbed to a pillar base where all could see Him. His clear, rich voice rang out over the crowd in words directed to all the needy and sinful. A hush fell over the vast multitude. "In the last day, that great day of the feast, Jesus stood and cried, saying, If any man thirst, let him come unto me, and drink." (John 7:37) Many of the people, when they heard this beautiful invitation to fresh new life, said, "Of a truth this is the Prophet." Others said, "This is the Christ." Again the incident was possible only to one who possessed strange power. Indeed, only Christ could talk like this.

Apparently Jesus awed even the officers of the Chief Priests and Pharisees who were always hanging around but afraid to arrest Him. When the officers went back without Him those pious connivers in high places said, "Why have ye not brought Him?" The officers answered solemnly, obviously deeply moved, "Never man spake like this man." The Chief Priests and Pharisees angrily pounded the table. "Are ye also deceived?" they asked sneeringly. But they were not deceived. So great was the power and truth which flowed from Jesus that these tough men knew in their hearts that there had never been anyone like Him—and that's true, there hasn't been, ever.

Somewhere near where we now sit was the treasury, probably in the Temple itself. Jesus was teaching there one day when he spoke some words that became immortal. Perhaps they still tremble in the air of this place where they were first spoken. How incredibly fortunate were those who heard Him say, "I am the light of the world: he that followeth me shall not walk in darkness, but shall have the light of life." (John 8:12) The day the realization first came that I was at the very spot where this great statement was made, I found myself listening intently and deeply. Indeed, so great was my concentration that I felt I could almost hear the unmistakable echo of those words, not in the air about me, but in my own heart. I was forced then to ask Him to help me to be worthy of the gift of "the light of life."

One more scene before we pass on to other fascinating places in the Old City; and it's a most dramatic episode. Early one morning Jesus came to this temple area and as usual a big crowd of plain people gathered round Him to listen to His wonderful teaching. But our old eager friends, the scribes and Pharisees, were up early also and right on the job at their usual dirty work.

This time they had in tow a poor, unhappy woman whom they had surprised in the act of adultery, and they were all for stoning her to death. Moses had handed down a law that this was the thing to do. And these men were looking forward in their sadism to beating the poor soul to death by pelting her with rocks. She lay cowering on the ground, her flesh quiveringly awaiting the first hard thud of a bitterly thrown rock, then a hail of them pulverizing her to death. These so-called holy men stood, faces hard, hands upraised, clutching stones.

But first they were going to trap Him—at least so they thought. But He was pretty hard to snare, not because He was clever but because He had truth on His side. They asked Him what He thought should be done in this case, when the law commanded that the punishment be stoning. To their surprise, Jesus didn't answer but instead stooped down and wrote something in the dust. They strained forward to see the writing. What did He write? No one knows. Could He perhaps have written their own names and the names of women with whom they themselves had committed adultery? At any rate, He had them cold; He said quietly, "He that is without sin among you, let him first cast a stone at her." (John 8:7) That was all.

The author and his son-in-law, the Reverend Paul Frederick Everett, conduct Sunday morning services at the Garden Tomb in Jerusalem. The open tomb of Christ may be seen beyond the speakers.

In a silence that was deathlike, though scores of people were present, He stooped down and wrote again. Their faces blanched, they swallowed hard. Their poised arms fell limply; the stones dropped harmlessly to the ground. Then one by one they slunk away; made themselves scarce, so to speak.

Jesus looked up. Only the woman remained. "Woman," He said, as if in surprise, "where are thy accusers? Hath no man condemned thee?" "No man, Lord," she replied softly. And Jesus said unto her, "Neither do I condemn thee." The woman stood with tears in her eyes looking at Him. She had never seen His like before. "Go," He said kindly and she moved away. "And," He called after her and she half turned, "sin no more."

She disappeared down one of those crowded streets over there with the determination to live a new life; and now she had the power to do so.

14

With the Master
in Old Jerusalem

ONE OF THE THRILLS OF JERUSALEM, ONE THAT NEVER CEASES TO astonish this author, is that wherever we walk, He walked long before us. The actual ground which He trod, the paving over which He passed are of course at a level beneath the present streets, but it's the same environment that He knew. The landscape, the hills and the valleys surrounding the city must be much the same as when He saw them. And because of the tough resistance to change which seems to mark the East, we may assume, I believe, that contemporary street scenes would not be completely unfamiliar to Him were He to return in the flesh.

I love the streets deep in the Old City; actually they are narrow lanes impossible for motor traffic but alive with people and animals, too. I have often heard behind me the heavy padded footfalls of a well-laden camel and felt more than once against my shoulder the nose of a burdened donkey. Thronging humanity, many selling, some buying, not a few sitting and lots of people just looking, fill the covered streets through which long broken shafts of sunlight filter. Like the bazaars of Damascus, the atmosphere is redolent with mingled aromas of cooking food, roasting meat, aromatic spices, indeed everything that smells good, with an occasional vagrant odor that is not quite so good. The total effect is one of vibrant aliveness and absorbing interest.

Little shops, some of them not more than ten by fifteen feet, are tightly wedged together on both sides of the narrow way. Proprietors sit cross-legged on bales of brightly colored material or atop burlap bags of grain. The more enterprising merchants stand outside their shops and smilingly endeavor to inveigle you inside. Often more than one will implore you at the same time, and a big babble ensues. But once you select a merchant and enter his shop, the others desist with joking and laughter, and all is quiet among the competitors. In every shop the very first act will be to serve you with black Turkish coffee in little china cups. Always the cups are exquisite. Many Americans do not like this coffee, but I do, and on every trip when I reach the area where it is proffered, I know that I am back in the Middle East which I love so much. And you must never refuse, or if you feel you must, then be extremely apologetic in doing so, for it is the symbol of hospitality, and a sip or two covers the amenities.

At intervals along these narrow streets you will hear Arabic music pouring from radios in little restaurants where men linger over coffee cups—genial souls, experts in leisure and relaxation. Indeed, taken by and large, Arabs are lovable people, sometimes complex, sometimes simple in nature. One thing is sure—they are superior in the old attractive virtues of simple friendliness and hospitality. Courtesy still lives except where crass and Western so-called culture has put its blight upon it.

The people on these narrow streets represent many contrasts and add infinite variety to the charming and fascinating street scene. Though many men are in Western dress with no coats and white shirts open at the neck, many women wear the long black dress, with veils just below the eyes. Older men, coated, still wear the red fez, and you may even see the big pantalooned trousers reminiscent of the Turks who ruled in Jerusalem for four centuries.

The cosmopolitan character of the crowds—black, brown, white faces, the snatches of many languages—reminds you that this is the great metropolis of religion, a city sacred to pilgrims from everywhere. But it is not merely a center of antiquity, for a surging present and beckoning future join hands with an enthralling past to make Jerusalem, Jordan, one of the most interesting cities in the world.

And of course in Jerusalem, as in all the Holy Land, we are constantly seeing evidences of that charming contrast of antiquity and modernity, which adds color and delight to our visit. This contrast of the old and the new in the Holy Land and the philosophical imperturbability with which people accept it as part of life, and nothing to get excited about, was particularly illustrated at the airport.

Here an airstrip is bisected by a highway, and a traffic light controls both airplanes and motor cars, as well as flocks of sheep and camel trains. One day at this intersection I saw an aged Arab in the old garb, leading a string of camels. He paused for a red light while a plane taxied in.

Without seeming at all interested in the plane, and gazing enigmatically ahead, he waited patiently until the light changed, then moved off leading his camels toward the desert. It was about the least concern with so-called civilization I have ever witnessed.

But while I always find the street scenes fascinating, there are a few spots in and around the Old City which to me have special meaning, and I would like to take you to them. One is the Pool of Bethesda, where I go to pray for all the sick who are in my ministry, praying that the Master Healer may touch all with the healing grace of the Lord Jesus Christ, as happened to a man here long ago.

A short distance inside the city wall from St. Stephen's Gate we walk through the lovely and tranquil garden of the Church of St. Anne. This noble and unique crusader church was built during the Latin Kingdom upon the remains of a Fifth-Century shrine that is supposed to mark the birthplace of Mary, the mother of Jesus. The crusader style of building is very evident in this church, with diagonal stone-cutting and Gothic arches.

Here within a compound lies the Pool of Bethesda, first excavated in 1876 and where extensive work is now in process. The pool is perhaps 20 feet below the present ground level, but one can go down to it. This is only a part of the original; the rest is still below ground.

Excavations at the Pool of Bethesda show its depth below the present street level. Around it in the time of Christ were commodious roofed porches supported by columns thirty feet high. The porches were filled with a multitude of infirm people who hoped to be healed by the waters. This was the scene of a fascinating story of a healing by Jesus. (John 5:1-9) Remains of Byzantine and crusader churches may be seen.

A portion of the Pool of Bethesda is built over by ancient arches.

The pool was composed of two huge tanks of water fed intermittently by a spring. Around it were five porches with arched roofs supported by colonnaded columns 21 feet high. The water in the pool was supposed to have healing properties, especially at those times when it bubbled— a phenomenon which we now know was caused by intermittent action of the spring. It was thought that whoever first got into the water at the moment of bubbling would be healed. St. John tells us about it: "Now there is at Jerusalem by the sheep market a pool, which is called in the Hebrew tongue Bethesda, having five porches. In these lay a great multitude of impotent folk, of blind, halt, withered, waiting for the moving of the water. For an angel went down at a certain season into the pool, and troubled the water: whosoever then first after the troubling of the water stepped in was made whole of whatsoever disease he had." (John 5:2-4)

The fact that the troubling of the water may be explained by natural cause does not in any sense detract from the great spiritual truth which Jesus taught on this spot where we now stand. For here the Master demonstrated in a most inspiring and thought-provoking way how His power and insight change defeated individuals into persons who thereafter live victoriously.

Jesus would naturally visit the great colonnades around the Pool of Bethesda, for wherever human need was, there He was. With pitying and loving eyes He saw the great crowd of "impotent" people lying there in varying degrees of hopelessness. The word "impotent" seems indeed well chosen, signifying ineffective people who had lost even the thought that they could help themselves, and were pathetically putting their faith in the agitation of water in a pool. Indeed, some did not even have the force to get into the water.

Such was the case of one man who had been futilely lying around the pool for 38 long years, the oldest old-timer among this motley crowd; and as such had no doubt a kind of prestige among these poor souls. In modern expression, he had become, through length of impotence, the big shot of the Pool of Bethesda. Jesus saw through him at once. His illness was probably psychosomatic, an escape from life, and he had lived thus for so long that he actually thought he was a very sick man, which perhaps is about the same as being sick. Possibly Jesus had previously noted this character and decided to lift him out of himself and his defeat into newness of life.

Accordingly, Jesus looked down at him where he lay on his pallet. The man became aware of a Presence. Someone was looking at him. Slowly he lifted his heavy-lidded eyes and immediately was caught up in the power that snapped from a pair of the kindliest, yet strongest eyes ever in a human body. The look from those eyes seemed to cut straight into that shriveled center deep within himself where he had withdrawn. Self-revelation resulted and he began to see himself for the faker that he was.

Jesus, the consummate Healer, with whom psychiatry and psychology haven't caught up, wasted no words. He hit the nail right on the head. "Wilt thou be made whole?" He asked, meaning "Do you really want to be healed?" But the fellow made an effort to stay within the prison of himself and began to whine, saying in effect, "Yes, of course I would like to be healed. Who wants to remain this way? But you see I have had such bad luck, for every time the pool is troubled, someone else gets in ahead of me, for there is never anyone to put me into the pool." Of course the Master did not go for this weak excuse. Surely, at least once in those long 38 years his chance would have come. If there was no other way, he could lie right at the edge and just roll in the minute the bubbling started. No, it was quite evident the man was deluding himself; he did not want to give up his poor, shabby prestige as the long-time sickest among the sick at the pool.

Again Jesus fixed His eyes on him. "Wilt thou be made whole?" He demanded. Suddenly the self-delusion of years fell away. The faintest hope stirred within the patient. Then Jesus said in that authority which He holds over all weakness, "Rise, take up thy bed, and walk." The man no longer hesitated, for the change had happened. He stood up, tested for a moment his flabby muscles, then picked up his bed and to the amazement of all strode through the colonnade and disappeared, a released, free man. What a smile there must have been on the face of the Great Healer as He watched him walk away into a new life.

One of the amazing facts in this incident is that this man did not know Who it was Who addressed him. Had he known that it was the famous Healer, Jesus of Nazareth, Who spoke to him, a psychological readiness for healing might have explained the result. But the story indicates that there emanated from the Master an enormous power that required no support of a preconditioned psychology. This incident describes the direct, uncomplicated application of the power of God bursting creatively into the mind and penetrating through a mass of barriers built up over many years to reach and heal a personality center. It was not until Jesus later encountered this man in the Temple that the latter realized Who had healed him.

I always do some pretty forthright meditating at the Pool of Bethesda, asking myself if I am holding back from the complete change of life which He promises those who surrender their lives to His direction. And always I give thanks for the amazing and glorious truth that no matter how weak and defeated we may be we can become whole; we can be cured; we can have new and vibrant life. We, too, can walk away from our old failures, sins and weaknesses. So listen believingly like the man in the story, as He says to you, "Rise, take up thy bed, and walk" straight into new and wonderful life. (John 5:8)

After this tremendous spiritual lesson at the Pool of Bethesda we will do well to return to our hotel by way of one of the loveliest garden spots in this world. How many times I have felt a spiritual blessing there! This garden, outside the city walls, some 650 feet north of the Damascus gate, is believed by many to be the site of Jesus' tomb, from which He rose on Easter morning.

It was discovered in 1883 by General "Chinese" Gordon, hero of Khartoum. The General was sitting on the roof of the home of Horatio G. Spafford, father of Mrs. Bertha Spafford Vester (whose hospital for children is one of the most effective Christian institutions in the East). General Gordon suddenly perceived, clearly defined, a hill that looked for all the world exactly like a skull. Two small dark caves formed the eyes, a ridge made the nose and a lower aperture, together with the above-mentioned phenomena, suggested a face. The whole, including a rounded hilltop above, gave the clear impression of a skull. Could it be possible that this, rather than the elevation within the Church of the Holy Sep-

Gordon's Calvary, so-called from its discovery in 1883 by General "Chinese" Gordon, was first noticed from what is now the roof of the Spafford Memorial Hospital, then the home of Horatio G. Spafford, father of Mrs. Bertha Spafford Vester of Jerusalem. Note the outline of a skull. Many people believe that Jesus Christ was crucified atop this hill.

ulchre, might be Calvary? It certainly fitted the Biblical requirement of being outside the walls, at least the present line of walls, and its peculiar formation could indeed mark this site as the place of the skull to which they took Jesus for crucifixion.

General Gordon excitedly realized that if this were indeed Calvary, the tomb of Joseph of Arimathea must be nearby. Excavations revealed a tomb under the hill, which is now referred to as Gordon's Calvary. Of some three hundred tombs excavated in Jerusalem, many Bible scholars and archaeologists have tended to feel that this particular tomb best fits the type in which the body of our Lord might have been laid. The garden and tomb are the property of an English society, which maintains it as a screne and secluded place of worship and meditation.

I do not wish to enter into the ancient argument concerning the authenticity of this place or of the Church of the Holy Sepulchre. Dr. Melvin M. Payne tells us that the work of Dr. Kathleen Kenyon in Jerusalem in 1961 and 1962 indicates that the site of the Church of the Holy Sepulchre is authentic. I can only say that when I put that question to Miss Kenyon in Jerusalem, I did not feel that I received a direct, affirmative answer. H. V. Morton thinks that a place marked since the Fourth Century as Golgotha indicates a long continuing tradition which, *ipso facto*, should be conclusive. But a tradition can be a slender proof of anything, even over a period of much less time than the three or four hundred years involved in this consideration. He also thinks the Christians would have fixed the spot, regardless of the intervening destruction and rebuilding of a pagan city atop the sacred sites. But might it not also be that they should want to forget what to them could have been a place of horror, where their Lord met the death meted out to criminals? It was some time before the preaching of the Cross became sacred.

I visit the Church of the Holy Sepulchre and pray in the sacred places within the church, which is presumed to enclose the tomb and the hill and rock rent in twain. I do not quite share the feeling, expressed by Leslie D. Weatherhead in his book, *It Happened in Palestine*, that the Church of the Holy Sepulchre is "an awful place," but I can only say that it does not appeal to me. I could only wish that Constantine and his mother had let the spot alone so that Calvary might have stood stark against the skyline forever.

Hence, I go for my rededication to the other Calvary and its garden, and it may just be that this is the actual place. Weatherhead cites the evidence of a small stone discovered on the site of the Garden Tomb in 1924, which was declared by a learned German archaeologist to be a shrine stone of the goddess Venus. We remember that in A.D. 135 at the second Roman destruction of Jerusalem, the Emperor Hadrian built a temple of Venus over the tomb of the resurrection to desecrate it.

The Garden Tomb is maintained by good Christian friends of mine, the Reverend and Mrs. S. J. Mattar. Their spiritual earnestness and sensitivity make it indeed a place of peace and holy quietness. You pull a bell in the high wall, and one of the Mattar family admits you, leaving you in the garden with your own thoughts and prayers, unless you ask for their interesting tour and lecture. Sitting under the trees, the open rock-hewn tomb before you, the hill of the skull above you, the crucifixion, the passion and death of our dear Lord and His glorious resurrection seem nearer and more real than ever you have felt in your life before.

The Garden Tomb is situated just beneath Gordon's Calvary, outside the walls to the north of the Damascus gate. That this is a very ancient burial site is indicated by the fact that just behind the high wall is the extensive so-called "Tombs of the Kings." Note the trough in which a huge stone, now gone, was rolled to close and open the tomb. Some believe it was in this serene garden that Jesus rose from the dead on Easter morning.

It is in just such a place, early on a bright dewy morning, women came to the tomb only to find it empty. Here Mary could have been the first to see Him and hear Him speak. To this tomb Peter and John came running. From this place the Gospel of the Resurrection went out to the farthest ends of the earth. It is indeed a precious spot of benediction and peace—this Garden Tomb.

A genial friend of ours in the court-yard of the American Colony Hotel in Jerusalem holds a loaf of Taboun bread. This bread is probably of the same type used in the time of Jesus. It is leavened bread, from very coarse flour, darker than our white bread, but not as dark as whole wheat. It is made into a large, round, flat loaf, often manipulated in the air like pizza dough, and then thrown into the Taboun oven. A Taboun oven is formed by taking round stones and heating them to a white heat by a fire made from animal dung. When the stones are very hot, the bread is thrown on them and baked somewhat like a pancake. It is very uneven, for you can often see the irregularities of the stone baked into the loaf; however, it is most delicious.

And so, having visited the ancient bazaars in Old Jerusalem, the Pool of Bethesda, Calvary and the Garden Tomb, we emerge into the busy modern street and thoughtfully proceed back to the American Colony Hotel. There in the cool pleasant courtyard with its tinkling fountain, we hear from the mosque next door the haunting cry of the muezzin from the circular balcony high on the minaret. Cupping his hands to his face, his aged, though strong voice sends out the call to prayer to all Islam. In his chanting voice he cries in Arabic, "Allah is great—there is no God but Allah and Mohammed is his prophet—come to prayer."

And we do come to prayer, to our Christian prayers, for after dinner we all go to the beautiful Upper Room of the American Colony. There we read together from the Book that comes so alive in this place where it was first lived. In the circle of Christian fellowship, we sing together, "In the Cross of Christ I glory, towering o'er the wrecks of time." Our hour of prayer comes to a high point of inspiration and dedication in the singing of a hymn written by Mrs. Vester's father who came here long ago to serve the Lord in the Holy Land,

> When peace like a river attendeth my way,
> When sorrows like sea-billows roll,
> Whatever my lot, Thou hast taught me to say;
> "It is well, it is well with my soul."
>
> Tho' Satan should buffet, tho' trials should come,
> Let this blessèd assurance control,
> That Christ hath regarded my helpless estate,
> And hath shed His own blood for my soul.
>
> My sin— oh, the bliss of this glorious thought!
> My sin— not in part but the whole,
> Is nailed to His cross and I bear it no more;
> Praise the Lord, praise the Lord, oh, my soul!
>
> And, Lord, haste the day when the faith shall be sight,
> The clouds be rolled back as a scroll,
> The trump shall resound, and the Lord shall descend—
> Even so— "it is well with my soul."
>
> For me, be it Christ, be it Christ hence to live
> If Jordan above me shall roll,
> No pang shall be mine, for in death as in life
> Thou wilt whisper Thy peace to my soul.

In the faith of Jesus Christ it is indeed well with our souls.

The author and his wife stand in a Jerusalem, Jordan, street.

15

Who Can Walk
Where He Walked?

THROUGHOUT THIS BOOK WE HAVE BEEN WALKING WHERE JESUS walked, and it has been a privileged experience indeed. But now the walking becomes harder, tougher, infinitely more demanding. In fact, as we attempt to relive the Master's agonizing experience in those last hours of His earthly life, in which "His sweat was as it were great drops of blood" (Luke 22:44), we are forced to ask, "Who can walk where He walked?" At best we can only stumble humbly and reverently along the way over which He passed to Calvary. His words echo in our minds, "If any man will come after me, let him deny himself, take up his cross, and follow me." (Matt. 16:24)

Let us go to the Garden of Gethsemane in the evening. The stars that have looked down upon this ancient city for so long come once again to the sky in which is hung a crescent moon. The towering old gray walls of the Holy City are bathed in silvery softness, and the little leaves of the olive trees among which we stand brightly reflect the moonbeams. A panorama of lights marks the Old City within the walls and the New City without. Save for the occasional honking of an automobile horn and the far-off barking of a dog, the night is strangely silent; even the horns and the barking seeming to be muted. Balmy night though it is, a suggestion of chill is in the air. Could it perhaps be caused by the place and the night and the long memory of tragedy that lingers here?

We look through the trees across the Kidron to the high corner of the huge walls, beyond which tower the pinnacle of the Temple, and to Mount Zion beyond. There on that night before the crucifixion was an

Ancient steps ascend Mt. Zion from the Valley of the Kidron. They end near the spot shown in the courtyard of the house of Caiaphas, the High Priest. Jesus mounted these steps under guard of the soldiers who took Him in the Garden of Gethsemane.

upper room in which a supper was being held. Suddenly terrible words fell from the Master's lips, "One of you shall betray me." (Matt. 26:21-25) All were deeply shocked and saddened. "Lord, is it I?" each one asked, in acute awareness of the weakness of mortal man. When Judas asked, "Is it I?" the Master quietly replied, "Thou hast said," and the betrayer slunk from the room and from the glorious fellowship and into the infamy of history.

With his departure the place seemed cleansed and the fellowship deepened. In fact, so wonderful was it that we repeat the supper even now in our churches, calling it Holy Communion. Sacred and deeply meaningful is it to all believers. Though these men about Jesus hardly comprehend the events of that night, yet they sensed that a divine act trembled in the very air. Says St. Matthew, "And when they had sung a hymn, they went out into the Mount of Olives." (Matt. 26:30) The hour had come.

Let your imagination refocus the scene out of the mists of time, and you can visualize that little group of men who came down the path along the walls headed toward Gethsemane. They seem to have stopped for a moment.

A stocky, bearded man was standing in the path and waving his arms. We, of course, know who he was and what he was saying. Simon Peter was his name and he cried out in protest at the thought that he would ever betray his beloved Master. "Lord, I am ready to go with thee, both into prison, and to death," he cried. (Luke 22:33) He meant it, too, and Jesus knew that he meant it. But the Master also knew the pathetic con-

Altar of the Basilica of Gethsemane stands by the Garden. Behind the altar rail is the large rock, pictured here, on which Jesus agonized in Gethsemane on the night He was betrayed. The woman kneeling at the altar is Ruth Peale.

flicts in men's nature—this man and every man. In the kindliest possible manner He said, "I tell thee, Peter, the cock shall not crow this day, before that thou shalt thrice deny that thou knowest me." (Luke 22:34)

The group moved on in silence. Only the muted sounds of sandaled footfalls were heard along the path. But the big, bearded fellow, head low on his chest, doggedly followed close behind the tall stately figure of the Master. They crossed the Kidron and moved into the garden among the trees. Clouds drifted across the moon's face. Only now and then a fitful flickering light showed through. Darkness deepened. The blackest night of man's long and evil life was at hand.

Jesus moved apart, a stone's throw from them, and there knelt and prayed in His human agony. He returned presently to His bewildered and tired disciples, who instead of standing by to give Him support were sound asleep. But He wasn't angry; He understood. He looked down at them lovingly. When shamefacedly they awakened, He expressed some disappointment that they should have gone off to sleep, leaving Him alone in the crisis of His life. But He was ready now, calmly ready, and prepared for whatever was to come.

And it wasn't long in coming, for soon moving lights appeared along the Kidron. As they came closer, there was also the sound of clanking armor and rough voices in the night. When a detachment of soldiers appeared in the garden a familiar figure was leading them. Coming up to Jesus, he kissed Him, having previously arranged to identify the Man the soldiers wanted by this despicable method. "Judas, betrayest thou the Son of man with a kiss?" (Luke 22:48) was all that Jesus said. Then followed a momentary hubbub in which one of the disciples hacked off the right ear of the High Priest's servant; probably a glancing blow of a sword. But Jesus told His friends this wasn't the way He wanted it, and He healed the man's ear.

The soldiers then seized Him and led Him through the trees toward the Kidron brook on their way to the house of the high priest Caiaphas, which stood on a shoulder of Mount Zion. The frightened disciples had already made their escape, running wildly through the olive grove. And the soldiers let them go. It was only He they were interested in. But you have to give Peter credit. He didn't run very far. He turned back and at a safe distance followed the detachment. Afar off, to be sure, but still he followed. Despite his fear for personal safety, he stuck by in a pathetically loyal sort of way. But a bit later he really hit bottom in his uncertain discipleship.

We follow the Master and the soldiers and Peter skulking behind in the shadows. The path passes the pool of Siloam and then climbs rather steeply up a long flight of steps. These ancient steps are still in place, having been excavated several years ago, and we may actually mount them one by one, placing our feet where He trod on that cruel night long ago.

The soldiers led the Master into the house of Caiaphas, the ruins of which are now incorporated in the beautiful Church of St. Peter's in Gallicantu (or St. Peter's at Cock-Crow). If Peter, following from a distance, could have foreseen that some day he would be called a saint and that where the Palace of Caiaphas stood would be a church bearing his name, he would no doubt have been the most amazed man in the world. But then Jesus Christ has built His kingdom on some pretty unlikely people, including some of us, who, nineteen centuries later, try so feebly to walk in His footsteps.

It was now late at night and cold. There was a fire in the courtyard of the Palace of Caiaphas around which the soldiers and palace help were warming themselves. Peter, perhaps colder than anyone, pushed up to the fire, his cape muffled around him in an effort to conceal his face. A sharp-eyed maid studied him, then said, "This man was also with Him." Peter denied saying, "I know Him not." (Luke 22:56-57)

Presently another of the bystanders declared, "Thou art also of them." Peter again vigorously denied, saying, "Man, I am not." (Luke 22:58)

He continued to hang around, trying to make out what the muffled voices inside the house were saying, for he realized full well the seriousness of the situation faced by the Master. An agonizing hour passed. Then another man who had been studying Peter and his strange actions, noting his Galilean accent, grew more suspicious, and his suspicions became certainty. He confidently affirmed, saying, "Of a truth this fellow also was with Him: for he is a Galilean." For the third time Peter forcibly denied, saying, "Man, I know not what thou sayest." (Luke 22:59-60) Almost before his outburst ended came the crowing of a cock, distinctly heard through the still night air.

A door opened and Jesus emerged in the midst of the soldiers. He turned and looked at Peter with eyes full of love and pity; and then Peter remembered the words of the Lord. It was too much. He turned and ran from the place, weeping bitterly.

To me the house of Caiaphas is one of the most meaningful places in all the Holy Land, and I have come here many times with my wife and family and with parties of pilgrims. There is a profound spiritual quality in this lovely church and its surroundings which helps one to feel the Holy Presence in a special way. I like to sit in the courtyard of a hot noontime under the fragrant pine trees and gaze down that flight of steps and think about Him.

The Church of St. Peter's in Gallicantu is in the charge of the Augustinian Fathers of the Assumption, Godly men who reverently show you the dungeon in which our Lord spent much of that last terrible night. The stocks where prisoners were cruelly flogged may still be seen. No doubt the Master was beaten here, as were also Peter and John and others of the disciples later on.

One of the Fathers whom I have come to know is a lovable and radiant Christian, Father Bernardine. On each succeeding trip to Jerusalem I re-

Father Bernardine of the Church of St. Peter in Gallicantu, reads by candlelight from the Scriptures in a cell of the dungeon beneath the house of Caiaphas. Here Jesus was imprisoned throughout the night He was taken. Here, also, Christians were beaten in the stocks which yet remain. Crosses carved by prisoners show in the stone walls of the dungeon.

turn to the house of Caiaphas and visit once again with this rare soul, who has dedicated his life to the humble service of God. Each time, in the High Priest's dungeon, which is now a lovely little chapel, Father Bernardine, in whom is only love for his Lord and the Lord's children, has asked me to read from the Scriptures, and then has taken my hand as together we pray the prayer the Master taught us. It is a most affecting spiritual experience, one that has enriched my life and the lives of others who have come here with me.

We go next to Pilate's judgment hall, which was in the Antonia, a once vast fortress occupying the northwestern corner of the temple area. It stood on the site of the John Hyrcanus' fortress Baris, which was rebuilt by Herod and renamed Antonia in honor of Mark Antony. Here Jesus was judged by Pontius Pilate. Today the site is Station Number One of the Via Dolorosa, or Way of the Cross. This sorrowful way led from the Praetorium at the Castle Antonia up the steep road to Golgotha outside the city walls, the place where criminals were executed and where Jesus died between two thieves. Every Friday pilgrims retrace the route over which Christ carried His cross.

On the site of the Praetorium stands the Franciscan Convent of the Flagellation where Jesus was flogged by Roman soldiers and where Pilate washed his hands after condemning Christ to death on the cross. Also on the site is the Convent of the Sisters of Sion, beneath which are well-preserved portions of the ancient Roman pavement of the Praetorium. Deeply scratched and diagrammed in the paving stones are games which the soldiers played to while away the time. Here they might have cast lots for the Lord's garments. And here also may be seen the vast and deep cisterns of the Antonia, which give one an awesome conception of the size and grandeur of the ancient fortress. There are huge blocks of fallen stone, smashed no doubt from the superstructure of the fortress by the battering rams of Titus when the city was destroyed in A.D. 70.

Spanning the Via Dolorosa is the Ecce Homo Arch, the remaining middle arch of a triple gate built by Emperor Hadrian. The name memorializes an episode in the trial of Jesus which was actually a kind of unconscious tribute paid the Master by His judge, the Roman procurator Pontius Pilate. This cynical politician, out of years of experience, had learned to know men very well indeed. He was quite able, I should think, to separate real men from false, and while he understood the latter better than the former, his shrewd perception enabled him to know at once a great and noble character when he saw one. The statement, "Ecce Homo" (Behold the man!) (John 19:5) was not merely an identification, but also a recog-

The sturdy towers of the Citadel of Jerusalem rise above surrounding buildings. These towers were left standing by Titus, but were dismantled and rebuilt by Hadrian. The Citadel was restored by Saladin, but in their present form the towers date from Suleiman the Magnificent (1540-42). The Citadel stands in part on huge masonry adjoining the site of the Palace of Herod the Great. Lord Allenby, entering the city on foot after conquering the Turks (he would not ride into the city where our Lord bore the Cross), read his proclamation from a platform of the Citadel to a great multitude welcoming British rule after four hundred years of the Ottoman Empire.

nition by Pilate that his prisoner was the most extraordinary man he had ever met in his long and checkered career.

We walk the Via Dolorosa, stopping particularly at the spot where Simon of Cyrene took up the cross for Jesus. Then we go on to the site of Calvary. It is the way of blood-stained steps of suffering. Finally we return to that peaceful garden under the lee of "a green hill far away, outside the city walls." Here in our evening worship we sing in a deepened spirit of dedication the hymn, "Must Jesus Bear the Cross Alone?" I am sure we shall resolve with dedication to help Him carry that Cross in the life of our own day and age, until the kingdoms of this world shall become the Kingdom of our Lord, and of His Christ, and He shall reign forever.

16

In Fabulous Judea
and Samaria

WITH WHAT EXCITING ANTICIPATION THE CHRISTIAN PILGRIM goes to Bethlehem. Since childhood this Judean town has been tenderly enshrined in consciousness. It is of the deepest inheritance of life. As the traveler takes the splendid highway from Jerusalem to the ancient city of David, he is almost sure to find himself humming the dear old words: "O little town of Bethlehem, How still we see thee lie!" And soon we do see it lying serenely on its hills humbly proud that the greatest event in human history occurred within its bounds. No other little town in all the world is so well known or more greatly beloved even by those who have never seen it.

The original name of Bethlehem, Ephrathah, meant "fruitful"—from the variant countryside centering there. But Bethlehem is perhaps more picturesque from a distance than in close-up. The town itself, while it is full of polite and friendly people, is to me, at least, somewhat less than satisfying. And this may be said of the Church of the Nativity built over a large cave where, in the section reserved for livestock, Jesus Christ was born.

When we are told that the Master was born in the stable of an inn, the reference is not to a Western type of barn, but rather to a large and extensive cave in which there were many smaller caves or "rooms." Even today families live in the many caves that may be seen along the hillsides; and their cattle, goats and sheep are also bedded down at night within the cave-home. On that immortal night when the weary Mary and Joseph arrived at the Inn in Bethlehem, only the part of the cave where the livestock was kept was available, because of crowded conditions.

115

This street scene in Bethlehem is viewed from Manger Square on which stands the Church of the Nativity.

The first Church of the Nativity was built over the cave or inn by Constantine and his mother Helena in the Fourth Century. After its destruction, some historians think in a Samaritan revolt, it was built anew by Justinian in the Sixth Century and restored at other times across the years. Originally three doors opened into the church, but two of them have been walled up and the remaining one reduced to a small opening to prevent camels, horses and donkeys from entering the basilica. One must stoop to enter. In the church are three altars, the high altar belonging to the Greek Orthodox, the altar to the left to the Armenians and that to the right also to the Greek Orthodox.

We descend two flights to the Grotto of the Nativity, where a silver star set in the floor marks the actual site of the birth of Jesus. Around it is the inscription *Hic de Virgine Maria Jesus Christus Natus Est* (Here Jesus Christ was born of the Virgin Mary). Sixteen silver lamps are always

This view of Bethlehem is from a balcony high on the Church of the Nativity. Still higher up in this tower are the famous bells whose deep-throated melody is heard around the world on Christmas Eve.

burning; six belong to the Greek Orthodox, four to the Latins and six to the Armenians. I was deeply moved on one occasion when a group of us, Americans, spontaneously started singing together a verse of the hymn "O Little Town of Bethlehem." The singing was followed by a simple prayer. It rather counteracted the unsatisfying character of the place and, I felt, brought the simple and humble Jesus nearer to all of us.

Always upon emerging from churches built over holy sites, which despite their devout intent often serve to confuse and sometimes even to repel the earnest pilgrim, I confess to a sense of relief. In the bright sunlight I find myself looking around at the hills and valleys that Jesus knew so well and am glad that He who said "I am with you alway" (Matt. 28:20) walks the open roadway with me.

So we go now a little more than a mile to the village of Beit Sahur beyond which, amidst olive groves, is the Shepherds' Field. Here simple shepherds "keeping watch over their flock by night" (Luke 2:8) were granted an immortal experience when the star-studded heavens were filled with the singing of a heavenly host "praising God, and saying, Glory to God in the highest, and on earth peace, good will toward men." (Luke 2:13-14)

A silver star set in a marble floor in the Church of the Nativity marks the spot where Christ was born. Around it is the inscription "Hic de Virgine Maria Jesus Christus Natus Est." (Here Jesus Christ was born of the Virgin Mary.)

It was here in this very area that an angel made to them the glorious announcement of the birth of their Saviour in nearby Bethlehem. Why to them, we wonder as we stand here? Why not to crowned heads, to the great of this earth? Perhaps the good tidings of great joy were deliberately given to men simple enough to accept truth that more complicated and sophisticated minds might reject.

A little farther on in an enclosure owned by the YMCA is an ancient cave excavated from the drifting sands of centuries. Its blackened roof shows clearly that it was used as a human habitation from early times.

This ancient cave lay for centuries beneath the sand in the Shepherds' Field. It might have been the spot where the shepherds "keeping their flocks by night" heard the Heavenly Host. It is owned now by the Jerusalem YMCA.

This cave is a rather good example of a place of many rooms. It might very well have been used by the shepherds as they kept watch over their flocks by night. At any rate it is now called the Shepherds' Cave.

The fertile plain nearby the Shepherds' Field is called the Field of Boaz and here occurred one of the most beautiful stories in the Bible, the story of Naomi and Ruth and Boaz. Naomi, wife of Elimelech of Bethlehem-judah, went to live in the land of Moab (through which we passed enroute to Jerusalem). The couple had two sons who took wives of the women of Moab. They were named Orpah and Ruth. Elimelech and the two sons died, leaving widowed the three women. The mother-in-law, Naomi, decided to go back to her own kinfolk in Judea and urged her two daughters-in-law to remain with their own people, letting her return alone to Bethlehem-judah. Orpah kissed her mother-in-law fondly and departed to the home she had left to marry Naomi's son.

But Ruth would not leave her mother-in-law, for she truly loved her and it was not in her loyal nature to depart from one so beloved. She expressed her love and devotion in words that for sheer lyrical quality are hard to surpass. "Intreat me not to leave thee, or to return from following after thee: for whither thou goest, I will go; and where thou lodgest, I will lodge: thy people shall be my people, and thy God my God: Where thou diest, will I die, and there will I be buried: the Lord do so to me, and more also, if ought but death part thee and me." (Ruth 1:16-17)

So the two inseparable women, the older and the younger, journeyed back to this place and in these fields Ruth gleaned after the reapers of the rich farmer Boaz. He became enamoured of her beauty of face and character and she became his wife. And the child born of this union and who was cradled in the arms of the loving Naomi was ancestor to the great King David.

Other excursions from Jerusalem, which I never fail to take, include a trip to Samaria. All along this route are the footprints of Jesus and the great men of the Old Testament. On our way we pass El-Bireh, some ten miles out. It was here that the parents of the 12-year-old Jesus, having gone a day's journey on their return trip to Nazareth, missed the boy and were forced to return to find Him. He was in the Temple disputing with the learned doctors. El-Bireh has for generations been a resting place for caravans from Jerusalem to Galilee and could indeed be where the parents of Jesus stopped for the night.

This watchtower is in a vineyard on the road to Samaria. Here the owner of the vineyard and his family lived during the period of ripening and harvesting of grapes in order to protect his crop from robbers.

My wife found this shapely jar in the watchtower in the vineyard as we passed by on our way to Samaria. She placed it in the sun and it seemed to make an interesting picture, typically Bible Land.

We go on to Bethel known and beloved by every student of the Old Testament. The night Jacob spent there is related in words of sheer music.

> And Jacob went out from Beersheba, and went toward Haran. And he lighted upon a certain place, and tarried there all night, because the sun was set; and he took of the stones of that place, and put them for his pillows, and lay down in that place to sleep. And he dreamed, and behold a ladder set up on the earth, and the top of it reached to heaven: and behold the angels of God ascending and descending on it. And, behold, the Lord stood above it, and said, . . . I am with thee, and will keep thee in all places whither thou goest, . . . And Jacob awaked out of his sleep, and he said, Surely the Lord is in this place; and I knew it not. And he was afraid, and said, How dreadful is this place! This is none other but the house of God, and this is the gate of heaven. And Jacob rose up early in the morning, . . . And he called the name of that place Bethel . . . (Genesis 28:10-19)

I have visited the excavations at Bethel, which have been carried out under the direction of Dr. James L. Kelso, and was present on the day pottery from the Abrahamic era was found at the foot of a deep and very ancient wall, the perfect joining of which seemed to me a marvel of construction. I saw the patriarchal high place of sacrifice which still shows bloodstains on the altar after the passing of thousands of years.

Our journey continues through the Valley of Robbers called Wady el-Haramiyeh and then into a verdant and lovely valley rich in olive and citrus groves. We turn off for a look at Shiloh, modern Seilun, where Joshua divided the land among the children of Israel. Shiloh was probably destroyed by the Philistines who burned it, as the excavations seem to indicate. Going on through country every inch of which is replete in Biblical history we pass a picturesque watchtower in a vineyard, where families keep watch over their ripening grapes lest the vineyard be plundered.

Near here is a village called el-Luban, the ancient Lebonah. In the Book of Judges (Chapter 21) we read an interesting story of how the sons of the tribe of Benjamin captured wives for themselves. The men of Israel had sworn they would not give their daughters in marriage to this tribe, but the Benjaminites outsmarted them. There was a yearly feast scheduled in Shiloh "in a place which is on the north side of Bethel, on the east side of the highway that goeth up from Bethel to Shechem, and on the south of Lebonah" (Judges 21:19)—in other words, right in the neighborhood through which we are traveling.

The young women of Shiloh came out during the feast and danced. Knowing this the young men of Benjamin lay in wait in the vineyard, perhaps this very one. When the opportunity came they dashed out and each captured a girl and carried her off squirming, but perhaps not too squirming, and married her. Well, that's one way to get a wife.

Proceeding, we rise to a high elevation over a marvelously engineered and perfectly graded highway, and suddenly spread out before us like the garden of the Lord lies the land of Samaria. Mount Gerizim rises on the left and beyond that Mount Ebal, and in the hazy distance to the north snowcapped Hermon seems to float in the still air. Down below in a vast valley lies ancient Shechem (modern Balata) and Sychar and the large modern city of Nablus.

Shechem was one of the strategic cities of antiquity, because of its location in the center of the pass across Samaria from the Jordan valley to the seacoast. The fascinating excavations which I have had the pleasure of visiting under the guidance of my friend Dr. O. R. Sellars, distinguished Bible scholar and archaeologist, revealed the massive walls and enormous gates of an elaborate defense system. The mightiest Bronze Age fortress of Palestine was found in Shechem. The great temple was built around 1600 B.C. and was in use until approximately 1200 B.C. Four hundred years later, or about 800 B.C., a granary was built over the temple. Shechem declined following the founding of Samaria by Omri, 5½ miles to the northwest.

Coins found at Shechem bear the inscriptions of Alexander the Great, and of the Ptolemies of Egypt. The size of houses uncovered, an oil extraction plant and high-quality pottery bowls indicate that an important and prosperous city once stood where these mounds have covered its remains for centuries. Among the great events that occurred in this now silent city was the assembling of a vast multitude here to offer the throne to Rehoboam after the death of Solomon. Where lizards now run among the stones one can almost hear the shouts of the people, the sounds of cymbals and trumpets, and visualize the pomp and ceremony.

We quench our thirst at Jacob's Well and while resting here ponder the beautiful lessons so forcibly yet gently taught by Jesus to the mixed-up and sinful woman from nearby Sychar when she came to draw water. (John 4:5)

Towering above us here (and the view from its summit is breath-taking) is Mount Gerizim, holy mountain of the Samaritans. When the Jews returned from captivity in 538 B.C. they found Samaritans intermarrying with Gentiles and angrily repudiated them as no longer Jews. The Samaritans therefore built a temple on Mount Gerizim in rivalry to the Temple at Jerusalem, and the two nations had no further dealings with each other. Meager ruins of the Samaritan temple may still be seen. The Samaritans, now numbering only some 200 persons living in their own section of the thriving city of Nablus, still perform their ancient religious ceremonies atop their holy mountain.

On our way to Sebaste, the Biblical city of Samaria, we pass Tell-Dothan which is said to be the place where Joseph (who had the coat of many colors) was sold by his jealous brothers to some Ishmaelite traders, who in turn sold him into slavery in Egypt. But the little scheme backfired. Joseph became the great man of Egypt, a fact that later became beneficial to the brothers, as Joseph instead of being revengeful saved all their lives during the great famine.

Sebaste, 50 miles north of Jerusalem, is the site of the capital of the Northern Kingdom and was built by King Omri in the Ninth Century B.C. It has a history of great magnificence, and although now in ruins (some of its glorious pillars have been used in the erection of ordinary houses in a rather poor village) it still retains a melancholy grandeur. The city enjoyed a wonderful defensive location, standing on a rather precipitous hill rising three hundred feet above a vast plain.

Many invasions were made against the city of Samaria by the then great powers. However it survived for nearly 200 years as the capital of the Northern Kingdom, until it was destroyed by Sargon of Assyria in 721 B.C. Several revivals took place until finally the city was presented to Herod by Caesar Augustus and renamed Sebaste (Sabastos being the Greek for Augustus). Herod made it a city on the grand scale, erecting the usual stadium, tribunal and theater. The forum, now used as a threshing floor, was once a magnificent city center surrounded by noble structures of which a line of pillars serve as reminders of departed glory.

These are the columned remains of the Temple of Kore built by Herod the Great on the summit of the hill where once stood the magnificent capital of Samaria, destroyed by the Assyrians in 722 B.C. Through the columns may be seen the Roman forum which is now a threshing floor for Arabs of Sabasti.

I have wandered beyond those pillars up through an olive grove to the ruins of the palace of King Ahab and gazed in wonder at the colossal colonnaded avenue running from the plain to the western gate of the once walled city. Well-preserved towers add to the impression of imperial power and elegance.

Something of the quality of life which went on in this place is illustrated by the story of King Ahab and his queen Jezebel. She must have been quite up to date, for we are told (II Kings 9:30) that she painted her eyes and attired her head. These two characters ruled in Samaria and apparently wanted everything their own way. Ahab, who possessed just about all any man, even a king, could expect, got his avaricious eye on the rich vineyard of a neighbor, one Naboth. This fine land lying near the Royal Palace in the valley of Jezreel afflicted the King with covetous desire. He took the matter up with Naboth, his subject, offering to exchange another vineyard for his property, saying he wanted it to further beautify his palace grounds. Or, if Naboth preferred, he would pay him money for his property. But Naboth, a sturdy fellow, did not want to give up his vineyard, as it was inherited from his father. He took pride in his ancestral lands and wanted to keep them.

King Ahab was really upset by this refusal and in fact went to bed and in a fit of pouting turned his face to the wall. He refused to eat and lay in tearful frustration because he could not have what he wanted. Then the real villain enters the story. Queen Jezebel came and sat on the bed and said, "What's the matter, that you won't talk to anybody or eat your supper?"

Then he blundered out the sad story to his "gentle" queen, how that inconsiderate Naboth just wouldn't cooperate. Jezebel was properly indignant and asked, "Aren't you the King of Samaria? Where does this fellow get off denying the King his desires!"

Not being able to stir him up even with this scathing approach, she decided to take care of the matter on her own. So she wrote a letter to the big men of the community in which Naboth lived and told them to put on an affair in honor of Naboth. She further advised that a couple of henchmen would get up at the right minute and denounce Naboth as traitorous to God and the King. (Funny how they always link God and king together.) Then they, the big men, were to up and kill Naboth just like that.

Well, what could they do when they got direct orders from the Queen? So they followed instructions and put an end to Naboth. Then Jezebel went to the King and told him all was just fine now, Naboth was dead and he had only to take possession of the coveted vineyard. Ahab was pleased just like a child who had gotten what he cried and pouted for.

But it wasn't all sweetness and light—no dirty work ever is. Elijah the prophet appeared in the late Naboth's vineyard and told the King that the dogs would lick up his blood and that Jezebel would be eaten by dogs. And that is just what happened. The story ends with dogs tearing to pieces the body of the evil Queen outside these walls—the ruins of which lie here in the sun and dust. It is just another demonstration of the inescapable fact that evil pays in its own coin. History surely does teach thought-provoking lessons.

17

Gibeon
and the Emmaus Road

ON OUR LAST AFTERNOON IN JERUSALEM, JORDAN, I WOULD LIKE
you to go with me first to the excavations of ancient Gibeon
(el-Jib) and then for tea at a German hospice, situated in a
serene and beautiful pine woods at el-Qubeibeh; one of our favorite places
around Jerusalem.

Going out from Jerusalem we admire the charming and elegant homes
being built along the Nablus road. The road follows an upgrade to Mount
Scopus and if you look behind you, and really you must do so, you will
see a magnificent panorama of Jerusalem, with the sun already beginning
to bring out those unforgettable pastel shades over mountains and city.

A conelike hill to the right of the road ahead is the site of Gibeah mentioned in I Samuel 10:26. Now called Tell el-Ful, it was excavated by
Professor W. F. Albright who brought to light Saul's Citadel, an uncouth
structure of dressed stone. It was here that Saul reigned as King, surrounded by his son Jonathan, his cousin Abner who commanded his army
and young David.

To the left is a far-off hilltop that marks Mizpah, where fortress walls
26 feet thick have been unearthed. These are the remains of a Judean
defense in the long feud between Jeroboam I and Rehoboam and between
Asa and Baasha. We also pass the birthplace of the prophet Samuel, the
village of er-Ram, or Ramah of Benjamin, mentioned in Joshua 18:25.
Along the way we see "the grass of the field, which today is, and tomorrow
is cast into the oven." (Matt. 6:30) It is actually a low bush that burns
easily with great heat.

126

Turning from the main highway onto a road leading to the left, we arrive at the picturesque village of el-Jib, site of long-lost Biblical Gibeon.

If you wish to read a fascinating and thoroughly enjoyable book, I suggest *Gibeon, Where the Sun Stood Still*, by Dr. James B. Pritchard, the archaeologist who excavated Gibeon at this site. Dr. Pritchard writes interestingly for the average layman as well as for the scientist, and the romance and excitement of his archaeological work comes through to the reader.

Excavations of Biblical Gibeon (el-Jib) reveal the ancient city wall built, circa 1200 B.C.

The village of el-Jib lies on a hilltop overlooking a wide, richly cultivated plain about 8 miles from Jerusalem and has an elevation of 2,500 feet above sea level. Here occurred one of the most dramatic and unusual events in modern Biblical archaeology, the discovery in the excavations of the actual name of the ancient city that was sought. The name of Gibeon was actually incised on a number of jar handles that were turned up in the dig.

The Gibeonites of old time were apparently a sly lot. Because of their desire to do business without interference from political turmoil, and because of their fear that the invading Joshua might murder them all as he did the inhabitants of Jericho, the Gibeonites devised a pretty clever trick to save themselves.

They decided they would go to Joshua and tell him a cock-and-bull story that they came from a far-off country. To convince him of this yarn they put old, ragged sacks over their donkeys, took wineskins along that were badly worn and many times mended, wore patched sandals and even carried stale and moldy bread. All of this was designed to indicate that they had come on a very long journey and not merely the few miles from Gibeon. The object was to trick Joshua into promising that he would not hurt them or their city if ever he came their way. And, believe it or not, Joshua fell for this bit of cunning and made a solemn covenant with them as requested.

When three days later Joshua learned that he had been tricked, he was really angry. But even so he stuck by his covenant. He would let them live, but he cursed them to the perpetual role of "hewers of wood and drawers of water" (Joshua 9:21), that is, menial workers. But that didn't seem to faze them as long as they would be unharmed.

However, the news of their deal with Joshua got out, and the King of Jerusalem, becoming alarmed at the disaffection of the Gibeonites, got four Amorite kings to help him lay siege to the fortified city of Gibeon to punish their citizens for desertion. The scared Gibeonites hastily sent a delegation to Joshua, this time undisguised, asking help and protection for an "ally."

In Joshua, Chapter 10, we read the account of the battle that ensued. "So Joshua came upon them suddenly, having marched up all night from Gilgal. And the Lord threw them into a panic before Israel, who slew them with a great slaughter at Gibeon. . . . And as they fled before Israel . . . the Lord threw down great stones from heaven upon them . . . and they died." (Joshua 10:9-11)

Here is a close-up of the excavation of an ancient city wall of Biblical Gibeon. Dirt is carefully removed in baskets to avoid possible loss of coins and other artifacts.

Then Joshua went all out. He spoke to the great round sun itself saying: "Sun, stand thou still at Gibeon, and thou, Moon, in the valley of Aijalon. . . . And the sun stood still, and the moon stayed, until the nation took vengeance on their enemies. . . . The sun stayed in the midst of heaven, and did not hasten to go down for about a whole day. There has been no day like it before or since, when the Lord hearkened to the voice of a man. . . ." (Joshua 10:12-14)

So, dear reader, mark this spot well. Here is the one place on earth where the sun, so we are told, actually stood still. You can just see Joshua standing here on this high hill imperiously raising his hand to the sun and thundering forth the command "Sun, stand thou still at Gibeon." Not content with that he also told the moon to stop over the valley of nearby Aijalon. What surprise there must have been among the heavenly bodies; but who were they to argue? Joshua was used to being obeyed and he meant business, so both the sun and moon stopped dead still— the first time that ever happened and the last time, too, at least to date.

The most spectacular feature found in the dig at el-Jib is a large pool with a passageway which the ancients had cut through limestone with primitive instruments to a depth of 80 feet. This excavated pool was filled with the debris of at least 60 generations. It had been cut originally to provide access to water deep within the hill, without exposure to attack from outside the walls. The huge cylindrical pool 37 feet in diameter and 35 feet deep has a spiral stairway with a balustrade of rock to protect water carriers ascending and descending. At the bottom of the pool the stairway continues into a tunnel for another 45 feet, opening into a water chamber 23 by 11 feet where good water still flows. The drama of archaeological excavation is indicated in Dr. Pritchard's description:

> Lying in the fresh water of the underground reservoir were two jars that had obviously been abandoned by the last users of this water system. To judge from their form and shape they could not have been made later than the first part of the sixth century B.C. If a water carrier had heard word shouted from above that the city wall had been breeched and that the enemy was within the gates, he would certainly have abandoned his jar in the water chamber and have fled up the seventy-nine steps in search of safety. Perhaps the two Gibeonites had done just this. The mute evidence of the two abandoned jars was sealed up when the conqueror closed the tunnel leading to the water with huge blocks of limestone pried loose from the city wall and pushed over the side of the pool to choke for 2,600 years the spring that had enabled the city to withstand siege as long as it did.

These steps lead down into the great pool of Gibeon, which figured in David's struggle for the throne after the death of Saul. The pool, cut from solid rock by the ancients, measures 37 feet in diameter and 35 feet in depth. At the pool's bottom, the circular stairway continues downward for another 45 feet to a marvelous continuous water supply referred to in the Bible as "the great waters that are in Gibeon."

As to the identity of the conqueror who filled the great pool we can only conjecture. Perhaps it was Nebuchadnezzar of Babylon who destroyed Jerusalem in 586 B.C., or possibly the Assyrian Sennacherib who entered Palestine in 701 B.C. and left an inscription boasting that he had conquered 46 Judean cities in his campaign. Maybe one of these was Gibeon.

This pool of Gibeon was the scene of a bloody affair. (II Samuel 2:13-16) It seems that 12 young men representing Saul and 12 representing David met by the pool. Each man proceeded to catch his opponent by the head and each thrust his sword into the side of the other, and they all fell down dead, which seems a stupid procedure. But then the battle grew, involving others, and David's men were victorious. Indeed this battle helped to determine the succession of David to the throne.

Excavations at Gibeon have shown that it was a center for the making and selling of fine wines. In the excavations were found jar handles inscribed with the name of the city and of persons, and a funnel and stoppers that fit the jar tops. A very large complex of presses and storage vats were also uncovered. Sixty-three vats cut out of the rock could accommodate enough jars to store 25,000 gallons of wine at one time. Jars filled with wine were stacked within the vats, which were found to maintain a temperature of approximately 65° F., a natural cooling system. The fact that the jar handles were marked with the name Gibeon and with the name of the producer seems to indicate that the town and the winemakers were known for a superior product.

Dr. Pritchard graciously guided our family through the entire dig, including the pool, the long tunnel leading to the spring outside the walls, the excavations of dwellings and the wine vats. He showed us a rather amusing evidence of human nature: one large wine vat contained a wall that divided it into two equal halves. It suggests, perhaps, a feud between two brothers over an inheritance which was seemingly solved by each taking his own half of the vat; only a supposition, of course, but an interesting one.

Many tombs have been excavated at Gibeon. One, labeled Tomb 15, is of particular interest. Dr. Pritchard's description of the opening of this sealed tomb, whose occupants had reposed there for 36 centuries, can hardly be improved upon:

> The first look was breath-taking. Here was an undisturbed sample of almost every aspect of the material culture of 3,600 years ago: storage jars, bowls filled with the residue of meat, lamps, perfume juglets, pitchers, dishes, weapons, jewelry, and the long graceful pins which had once held together the edges of a woven garment. With this rich assortment of articles of daily life which had been provided for the dead by their survivors, there were the bones and skulls of at least fourteen people for whom this tomb had been a peaceful home for thirty-six centuries. . . . Here for the first time a skeleton was found relatively undisturbed, lying on a bed of carefully placed white and black stones, surrounded by jars and bowls which had once held drink and food for the dead. Across the spinal column of the skeleton lay a beautifully preserved bronze dagger, which had once been attached to the belt which the man had worn.

In the corner of a room in one house of antiquity 23 coins of the period 103-76 B.C. were found buried. Some citizens of the time of Alexander Jannaeus had probably worked hard and scrimped and saved for that money. Whether he died without revealing its whereabouts or some disaster occurred, the fact remains that it lay buried until found by archaeologists 20 centuries later in 1956. So passes the life of mortal man.

We now travel on from Gibeon. The road which we follow from el-Jib (or Gibeon) to el-Qubeibeh traverses a countryside of special meaning. It was over an ancient rocky road, sections of which may still be seen near to the present one, that two followers of Jesus had a most significant spiritual experience. For el-Qubeibeh may very well be the village of

Emmaus on the road to which the resurrected Christ revealed Himself to two faithful men.

These two ardent followers, one Cleopas, the other unnamed, were walking the seven miles from Jerusalem to Emmaus late one afternoon. They were sadly talking together of the terrible events of the trial and crucifixion, when suddenly and apparently out of nowhere they were joined by another person who inquired why they were so sad and gloomy. They asked in surprise if he did not know about the death of the wonderful Teacher whom they and many others had believed to be the long expected Messiah. They further explained that it was now the third day since these events had occurred, and something very strange and exciting had happened. His grave was found empty and there were incredible reports that He was actually alive.

Then the Stranger, who exerted upon them an unusual fascination, began to explain the prophecy in the Scriptures relating to Christ; how the Messiah had to suffer and die before entering into His glory. The Stranger had a marvelous mind and a rarely gifted personality, and they were charmed by Him, so much so that when they reached Emmaus they urged Him to stop and have supper with them. As they sat at table He took the nut-brown bread in His hands and broke the loaf. Something in His gesture opened their eyes and suddenly they knew *Him:* and immediately He vanished out of their sight.

Forgotten was the meal and that night had fallen. They ignored the fact that the road was dark and perhaps dangerous by reason of robbers. Nothing made any difference. They were so excited that they rushed back to Jerusalem as fast as they could go to report to the others the heart-stirring fact that they had actually met Jesus Himself on the road; that He was indeed alive. (Luke 24:13-35)

The appearings and reappearings of the risen Christ, of which the Emmaus story is one, teaches us that along life's road that is often hard and painful Christ ever walks. And as we turn our thoughts to Him and love Him, He will break the bread of life with us also and restrengthen us in His service.

A woman gracefully carries a jar of water, a familiar sight in the Holy Land.

This clean Arab town near el-Jib has a mosque with graceful minarets, such as are seen all over Jordan.

So it is that we like to conclude our Jerusalem, Jordan, visits by going down the Emmaus Road on a bright and golden summer afternoon when glory, at once serene and lovely, lies upon the Judean fields and hills. Supping together in the quiet garden of the hospice something of the spiritual experience of Cleopas and his friend may be ours also.

But the experience of Christ's near Presence is not cheaply given. I have traveled this road many times without anything particularly happening, except enjoyment of the never failing peace and loveliness of the landscape. But one day my wife and I came this way with our dear friend Mrs. Bertha Spafford Vester, who is perhaps the oldest foreign-born resident of the Old City, having been brought to Jerusalem by her parents from America some 83 years ago.

Her hospital, the Spafford Memorial Children's Hospital, is truly one of the most humanitarian institutions I have ever known. She has saved the lives of hundreds of little children across the years. My wife is president of the American Colony Charities Association, the organization in the United States which collects funds to support this hospital.

On our drive this particular day we traveled very near to the border where we were stopped by soldiers at a Jordanian guard post. A burly sergeant sternly asked us where we thought we were going. Then he saw Mrs. Vester in the rear seat and immediately a smile spread over his face. Opening the car door he took her hands in his and kissed them. His entire attitude was one of love, even veneration. The other soldiers likewise crowded in to touch her hand. It was very moving to observe this little scene.

As we drove on, Mrs. Vester with her sweet smile explained, "The sergeant was one of my babies. He was brought to the hospital nearly dead. Through the Lord's help we were able to save his life. Pretty big and husky now, isn't he!" At that very moment, surrounded by such genuine human love, I had a strong and moving sense of the Presence on the Emmaus Road. Tolstoy was indeed right: "Where love is, God is."

18

We Meet
Samson and Goliath
in a Modern Land

WE BECOME VERY AWARE OF AN EMBATTLED BORDER IN CROSS-ing from Jordan into Israel. The crossing is made through the Mandelbaum Gate over a no-man's land some eight hundred feet wide which is closely guarded by Jordanian troops on one side and by Israelis on the other. Before the 1948 partition of Palestine, Jerusalem was one city. Now one observes that the clean street in Jerusalem, Jordan, suddenly runs into a grass-grown road crossing no-man's land, then begins spick-and-span again in Jerusalem, Israel. Houses in no-man's land stand starkly in bombed-out wreckage; mute evidence of the bitter shellfire that swept this area. Clashes still occur upon occasion, not only here, but elsewhere along the length of the border.

Our luggage is deposited at the Jordanian side of no-man's land and is carried by porters to the other side, where we go through passport control into New Jerusalem, so called in contrast to the Old City from which we came. Immediately we are aware that we have entered an atmosphere that is Western rather than Middle Eastern. In fact, Israel impresses one as a western state, perhaps almost an American one, pinned to the vest of the Middle East.

The energy and enthusiasm of people building a new country are very apparent. I wish that I had space in this book to describe the sociological mingling of people from many lands which has been admirably carried out here. I have visited a number of planned communities and have been greatly impressed by the intelligent manner in which lifelong residents of other nations have been integrated into a new national life. Fortunately for the Israelis, they have been well financed and this, together with their immense enthusiasm and intelligent approach to problems, shows clearly in the remarkable results achieved.

Since this book deals primarily with religious places and history, contemporary sociological investigation is only incidental to our main purpose. This fact makes it a bit difficult to describe properly the life of modern Israel, for the outstanding fact here is not its ancient Biblical association, but its dynamic building program.

We continue our tour of sacred Holy Land places by visiting the Coenaculum (Cenacle), Latin for dining hall. Here Jesus and His disciples observed the Last Supper. You will recall St. Mark's words: "And He sendeth forth two of his disciples, and saith unto them, Go ye into the city, and there shall meet you a man bearing a pitcher of water: follow him. And wheresoever he shall go in, say ye to the goodman of the house, The Master saith, Where is the guestchamber, where I shall eat the passover with my disciples? And he will shew you a large upper room furnished and prepared: there make ready for us." (Mark 14:13-15)

As previously pointed out, Jerusalem was laid waste on several occasions, even plowed over, but at this site on Mount Zion there can hardly be any doubt that we are standing on, or at least near to, the exact spot where this great event in Christian history, the Last Supper, took place. Moreover, it is believed that the vastly important event of Pentecost occurred here. "And when the day of Pentecost was fully come, they were all with one accord in one place. And suddenly there came a sound from heaven as of a rushing mighty wind, and it filled all the house where they were sitting. And there appeared unto them cloven tongues like as of fire, and it sat upon each of them. And they were all filled with the Holy Ghost." (Acts 2:1-4)

It was from this place that Jesus went to Gethsemane and to the crucifixion on Calvary. And it was here seven weeks after the resurrection that the power of God came in dramatic force upon these simple men, transforming them from ordinary human beings into flaming evangels. With the new faith burning like fire in their minds and hearts, they went out from the great Pentecostal experience to evangelize the whole world in the name of Christ. From this very spot Christianity began to spread like hallowed fire from heart to heart.

The great message was that death could not destroy Jesus. He was alive. And in Him we would live also. Look across those desert hills and valleys, for they were once swept by fire, the fire of the spirit. It caught men up and so filled them with spiritual power that ancient civilizations fell before their evangelizing zeal. And the fire continues to burn to this very day; now brightly, now dimly, but it has never gone out. God grant that it never will, that it may burn brightly in us in our time. We must hand on this holy fire to our children and our children's children, that the Kingdom of Christ may ultimately fill the world with goodness and love.

Also in this building is the tomb of the great King David. Since the Twelfth Century when the tomb was discovered, this site has been shown as David's last resting place. Rabbi Benjamin of Tudela, who came to Jerusalem in 1173, records that about 15 years earlier (1158) a wall of the church on Mount Zion fell, revealing the entrance to a cave. Workmen, thinking the cave might perhaps contain hidden treasure, entered and worked their way in until suddenly they were astonished to see a great palace. As they approached, a huge gust of wind surged through the cave crying with the voice of a man: "Rise and go hence, for God doth not desire to show it to man." So runs the fascinating story told by Zev Vilnay, the prominent Israeli historian.

If you wish to look into Biblical hell, you may do so from this point, for the valley or ravine of Hinnom lies before you. In ancient times it was a place of wickedness; of idols and infant sacrifice. It has always been pictured in terms of the abode of the wicked in the after life, and was called Gehenna.

After a magnificent panoramic view of the Old and the New Cities from the tower of one of the most beautiful YMCA buildings in the world, I want you to come with me to one of my favorite Biblical places, the valley of Elah. We travel through lovely country enroute. Wide, stately valleys and forest-covered hills provide vistas that are charming indeed.

On the way we pass through the romantic Samson country. In fact, the strong man is even immortalized at one crossroad, which is named for him. There, rather amusingly, stands an American-style hot dog and hamburger stand from the front of which is emblazoned "Samon's Café." Samson, who was born in this area some three thousand years ago at Zorah, ruins of which may be seen, might have turned out pretty well had he not fallen in love with an unscrupulous woman named Delilah from the valley of Sorek, and this proved to be his undoing.

If you have any doubt as to the ability of the Bible writers to tell a fascinating story, read Judges, Chapters 13-17, and believe me, doubt will vanish. It seems that an angel of the Lord came to the barren wife of Manoah, who lived in Zorah, and told her she would have a child whom the Lord wanted to use to overcome the Philistine domination of Israel.

But one thing was made clear—this boy's hair was never to be cut, for this was the secret of the phenomenal strength that would be his.

When Samson grew up, to the regret of his parents he fell in love with a Philistine girl, a daughter of the hated enemy. On his way to marry her a big lion attacked him on the road, but the lion didn't realize whom he was attacking, for this strong man grabbed the beast and ripped it in two with his bare hands. All went well for a while, then Samson and his wife fell out, because she double-crossed him by telling his enemies the answer to a riddle which she had wheedled out of him. Apparently women could do most anything to this rather dumb character.

This so annoyed Samson that he went down to Ashkelon, a seacoast town near here, and killed 30 men, taking their money to get the prize of thirty sheets and garments which he offered for solution of the riddle which his wife had given away. Samson went home to his parents for a while. Then, feeling kindlier toward his dishonest wife, he returned, bringing her a present. But he found that her father, thinking Samson had deserted her, had married the young wife to someone else. This irritated Samson, so he figured out a revenge on the Philistines.

The corn was standing tall and ready for harvest. Samson caught three hundred foxes and tied firebrands between the tails of pairs of them. He set the frightened foxes loose in the Philistines' corn, burning it, together with their olive trees. Angry because Samson's wife and father-in-law had caused him to do this, the Philistines burned both of them to death. To get even, Samson fell upon the Philistines and "smote them hip and thigh with a great slaughter." (Judges 15:8)

The Philistines then threatened the leaders of Judah because of the depradations of this strong man and told them they would have to bind and deliver Samson—or else. In seeming cooperation Samson let them bind him with new cords and they turned him over to the conquering Philistines. The latter thought they surely had him this time, but he flexed and bulged his enormous muscles, and snap—the cords flew off. Then just to show them a thing or two, Samson picked up the jawbone of an ass and with it killed exactly 1,000 men.

Then our bloodthirsty friend went down to Gaza, near here, to the house of a local harlot. His enemies heard he was there and put a guard around the house, ordering them to lie in wait until morning, when they would kill him. But he fooled them. He left the harlot at midnight, and on the way out of town, just for sport, picked up the city gates and carried them on his shoulders, setting them jocularly on the top of a hill near Hebron, which is now in Jordan about 25 miles away.

The next thing our hero did was to fall in love with the lady known as Delilah. The top men of the Philistines knew this girl and told her sweetly to beguile this strong boy and learn the secret of his strength, in return for which they would give her 1,100 pieces of silver. Samson strung her along for a while by telling her first to bind him with green withs and he would be weak. She did so and then cried, "The Philistines be upon thee, Samson." (Judges 16:9) But he burst these green withs as if they were nothing. She tried it again and this time he told her to tie him up with strong new ropes. Again she cried, "Here come the Philistines," and his muscles bulged and snap went the ropes.

Then the poor fool really fell for her wheedling ways and told her that his strength was in his hair, which had never been cut. So when he was asleep she snipped off his hair and called for the Philistines. Samson awakened and summoned his prodigious strength, but it was gone. He had become just an ordinary man. So the nice gentle Philistines gouged out his eyes, then took him into Gaza where they bound him with fetters of brass and made him grind corn in a prison house.

Time went on and his hair grew out again. The Philistines weren't any too bright in letting that happen. They decided to have a big feast in thanksgiving to their god Dagon, because he had delivered their terrible enemy into their hands. When they had gotten drunk and happy, the big crowd of lords and ladies sent for Samson to make sport of the blind giant. They put him between two pillars and laughed and catcalled at him. He asked the boy guiding him to let him feel the key pillars that held up the big banqueting house. This lad, never thinking, did just that. So Samson took hold of the two middle pillars upon which the house stood and said, "Let me die with the Philistines. And he bowed himself with all his might, and the house fell upon the lords, and upon all the people that were therein. So the dead which he slew at his death were more than they which he slew in his life." (Judges 16:30)

Quite a story, and it took place in this very territory through which we are traveling. It must have caused quite a lot of excitement in those days; indeed the Bible gives three whole chapters to the story. Lots of people, especially the remaining Philistines, must have been pretty happy when Samson was safely in his grave over there near Zorah in the family burial plot.

We come presently to the valley of Elah, another famous Biblical place where another giant made a name for himself. This valley spreads out between Azekah and Kefar-Zekharia, or as the Bible describes it, "between Shochoh and Azekah." The name *Elah* comes from the elah or terebinth

This brook in the Valley of Elah (photo taken in the summer dry season), is where young David took the stone which he used in his sling to kill the giant Goliath. The giant came from the hill in the background to meet his youthful opponent in this valley.

trees that grow on the adjacent hills. The valley stretches toward Bethlehem, David's home town, which is in Jordan but hardly more than twenty miles away. The historical era in which the valley of Elah figures in the famous story of David and Goliath was in the time of King Saul, approximately 1020-1000 B.C. The incident is described in I Samuel 17.

It seems that the Israelites were having a war with their old enemies, the Philistines, and the two armies were glaring at each other from opposite sides of the valley. But at the moment it was a peculiar kind of war they were having, for the armies were not clashing in combat. Instead, the Philistines had a big fellow whom the Bible calls a giant. He was the size of about three ordinary men, and he was dressed in armor and carried a spear as long as a telegraph pole. He would come out in the center of the valley every morning and make the Israelites a sporting proposition. In a voice like thunder, he would dare them to send down a man to fight him; if the man they sent killed him, the Philistines would give up and become the slaves of the Israelites and vice versa.

This was the catch, for the Israelites had no giant and the Philistines knew it. So he came out every day for 40 days and shouted his challenge up to the Israelites, who were both scared and impotent. Do you know that would not be a bad way to have a war—just let a few dictators and politicians and war profiteers fight it out while the rest of us sit up in the grandstand and watch the fun. As soon as those fellows heard the bullets whistle, they would forget all about being dictators, and would take to the woods; and you can rest assured there would be no more wars.

Well, to get back to our story, this giant, whose name was Goliath, tried this stunt of his just once too often. One day when he was shouting his challenge, a young lad, a shepherd from the hills, happened to overhear him. Now this boy was only average size, but his body was strong and clean, and his mind and soul were clean, too, for his conscience was clear of any bad business. He was no modern sophisticate, no washed-out character, this boy. He was real stuff, from the bottom of his feet to the crown of his head, and he did not know the meaning of fear. He said, "Let me at him, I will go down and fight this fellow from across the valley." And to the astonishment of all, he started toward the giant.

The giant saw him coming and noted that he had on no armor and carried no sword or spear, and he was insulted that a mere boy should dare to step up to him. With many loud threats he conveyed to this boy, whose name was David, that his body would soon feed the beasts of the field. David had a different idea. He stopped by a brook (and the brook is still here) and chose five round, smooth stones which he put into his pocket; that is, all but one, which he put into a slingshot. As he watched his sheep, night after night, he had practiced with this slingshot so that he had become expert. He said to the giant in effect, "You are very big and you talk loudly, but you are really very stupid, as stupid as all those benighted people who believe that brute force is strength."

The Bible in more classical language reports his remarks as follows: "Then said David to the Philistine, Thou comest to me with a sword, and with a spear, and with a shield: but I come to thee in the name of the Lord of hosts." (I Sam. 17:45) So saying, he twirled his slingshot and the stone sped unerringly toward his mark, hitting the giant in the forehead with a thud. The big fellow never had a chance to use his spear, for he fell to the ground, dead.

To finish it off in proper style, David went over and stood on Goliath's chest and, taking the giant's sword, cut off his head. Now, of course, that may have been going a bit far, but that is the way they did it in those days, which, after all, is better than dropping a bomb on innocent men, women and children. But that is beside the point which I want to convey, namely, that this boy, David, had what it took to meet this giant and to give him a good licking.

After two such rugged experiences out of the long past, it will rest us to drive to a beautiful Mediterranean seacoast hotel at Herzlia for the night. Enroute we stop for a look at the ruins of Askelon, which was one of the five most important cities of the Philistines in ancient times. It had a good harbor and was a center of culture. When King Saul was killed by the Philistines, David did not want his enemies to rejoice, and he mourned the great king, crying, "Tell it not in Gath, publish it not in the streets of Askelon; lest the daughters of the Philistines rejoice." (II Sam. 1:20)

From here to the border of Israel at the Gaza strip, where Egyptian territory begins, is only 6½ miles. We go north, however, to Tel Aviv through a rich plain of citrus groves. The highway is bordered by long avenues of eucalyptus trees planted within the past few years—and they are most attractive. We pass through Ramla, a pleasant town that is of interest to us chiefly because it is built on the site of Biblical Arimathaea, the home of Joseph, who took the body of Jesus after the crucifixion and placed it in his own tomb from which in the glory of Easter morning Christ rose from the dead.

On our way into Tel Aviv we pass the town of Lod or Biblical Lydda, referred to in the Gospels, "And it came to pass, as Peter passed throughout all quarters, he came down also to the saints which dwelt at Lydda." (Acts 9:32) The fine airport of modern Israel is located here. Peter wouldn't recognize the place. We hope some "saints" still dwell here. The city of Tel Aviv, now with a population approaching 500,000 people, was established on sand dunes adjacent to Jaffa hardly more than 50 years ago. It is a city of beautiful buildings and hotels, an amazing community in its growth, though personally I prefer the seaport of Haifa further north, which is a very fine city.

Jaffa can be seen in the background of this view of Tel Aviv and its busy seashore.

This is a Jaffa waterfront scene. In biblical times this ancient city, called Joppa, was the famous seaport which figured in the story of Jonah, who "rose up to flee unto Tarshish from the presence of the Lord, and went down to Joppa; and he found a ship going to Tarshish." (Jonah 1:3) Simon the tanner lived here and Peter stayed with him for many days. (Acts 9:43)

Jaffa, or Joppa as it is called in the New Testament, belonged to the tribe of Dan and has been an important port since the time of King Solomon. The harbor, one of the most ancient in the world, was mentioned by Hiram, King of Tyre, who told Solomon he would float the cedars of Lebanon by sea along the coast to Joppa, thence they could be carried to Jerusalem for the building of the Temple. And Joppa figures also in the story of Jonah who "rose up to flee unto Tarshish from the presence of the Lord, and went down to Joppa; and he found a ship going to Tarshish." (Jonah 1:3) I always look out to sea hoping to see a whale when I pass through Jaffa. Simon, the tanner, lived here and St. Peter stayed with him.

And so we come to Herzlia, named for Theodor Herzl, a famous figure in modern Israeli history. Here in a luxury hotel that might very well grace the southern Florida seacoast we dine, watching a full moon rise over the Mediterranean; and we sleep well in air-conditioned comfort.

19

To the Sea of Galilee

THIS WILL BE AN UNFORGETTABLE DAY, THE EXPERIENCES OF WHICH may affect your life forever. For today we shall visit the boyhood home of Jesus and other places sacred to His ministry. Of course, we are going to the Sea of Galilee.

The highway north parallels the Mediterranean shore through the beautiful plain of Sharon. Before turning eastward toward our destination Tiberias, we visit ancient Caesarea which was the Roman capital in Palestine for nearly five hundred years. Founded in 22 B.C. by Herod the Great it was named in honor of Caesar Augustus, Emperor of Rome from 27 B.C. to A.D. 14. Thus the town came into being shortly before Jesus' earthly life.

Judging from the extent of the ruins it must have been an important harbor city and one of considerable grandeur. Caesarea had a very large hippodrome that could seat about 20,000 spectators, and an impressive forum. Two colossal statues have recently been unearthed as well as large marble columns. In the hippodrome three large cone-shaped blocks remain. They were smoothly polished and shone very brightly like mirrors, as their purpose was to excite the horses in the races.

The city was important to early Christianity, for in the Fourth Century it was the home of the Greek Eusebius, one of the church fathers and an historian of note. The Holy Grail was said to have reposed in Caesarea. Made of glass, it was believed to be the same cup used by the Lord at the Last Supper. It was later taken by the crusaders to Italy and preserved under the name Sacro Catino.

St. Paul, after his conversion outside Damascus, went first to Jerusalem and then shipped out of Caesarea to his home city of Tarsus. Many years

This stone at Caesarea mentions the name of Pontius Pilate in the time of Emperor Tiberius.

later, following the attack on him in the Temple at Jerusalem, he was imprisoned for two years in Caesarea before being sent to Rome in A.D. 65, there to suffer martyrdom for the faith. Here in Caesarea is to be seen a rare stone inscribed with the name of Pontius Pilate, who occupied the Governor's residence.

The crusaders restored Caesarea in the Twelfth Century, though it appears that the crusader town was smaller than the Roman city had been. Recent excavations have uncovered the great rampart, or wall, long buried under the sand dunes. It is one of the most impressive medieval turreted walls and fortresses that I have ever seen, and gives an impression of grandeur as one stands upon the ramparts gazing out to the blue Mediterranean. History seems to tremble in the very air of this place, and I am always lured back to Caesarea by a mystic charm in which the ancient city seems to lie enshrined.

Great walls of Caesarea built by the Crusaders have been remarkably preserved for centuries under the desert sands.

Returning a bit south we turn at Hadera in the direction of Afula. This is a very historic road, the road to Megiddo. From ancient times the armies of Assyria and Egypt and other great powers have passed over this highway, the Via Maris. Lord Allenby, conqueror of the Turks, who took as his title *Lord Allenby of Megiddo*, marched his armies over it. As we enter the vast valley of Jezreel, encompassed by the mountains of Galilee, we come to the huge ancient tell, or mound, where stood Megiddo, one of the greatest fortresses of antiquity.

Megiddo was of strategic importance, situated as it was in a narrow pass controlling highways to the great centers of civilization. King Solomon levied a tax for the fortifications and had stationed there some 1,400 chariots and 12,000 horsemen. Excavations at Megiddo reveal large stables which bear out the statements in the Bible. (I Kings 9:15, 10:26-29; II Chronicles 1:14-17, 9:25)

In the valley of Jezreel stretching to the north and east, and which is also called the plain of Esdraelon, some of the great battles of Biblical history were fought. Here Barak and Gideon were victorious; here Saul and Joshua suffered defeat.

Here is a model of the great fortress of Megiddo at the time of its glory.

The frequency with which Megiddo was the scene of battles throughout history makes it a symbol of warfare. In fact, the New Testament envisions it as the site of the last great battle of mankind. In the book of Revelation (16:14, 16) we read, "For they are the spirits of devils, working miracles, which go forth unto the kings of the earth and of the whole world, to gather them to the battle of that great day of God Almighty . . . and he gathered

them together into a place called in the Hebrew tongue Armageddon."
The word Armageddon is a corruption of Har Megiddon, Hebrew for
"Mountain of Megiddo." We must consider that there is enough explosive
potential in this part of the world to give the prophecy a sinister significance.

We arrive presently at Nazareth, the boyhood home of Jesus. It lies in a
large cup among the surrounding mountains of Galilee. Coming into the
town we pass the "hill of precipitation," from which angry Nazarenes at-
tempted to throw Jesus after His sermon in their synagogue. But God
shielded Him and He walked through them. (Luke 4:28-30) On my last
trip I noticed that steam shovels are digging vast quantities of·stone from
this hill, using it as a quarry so that perhaps the hill, famous in Christian
history, may disappear altogether.

For that matter everywhere in this country along roadways where the
prophets and Jesus once passed, steam shovels dig, tractors plow and fac-

Huge conduits, large
enough to drive a jeep
through, will run un-
derground to take off
Sea of Galilee water for
irrigation purposes.

tories rise. Indeed, a few miles farther on I saw on my last trip a large
pumping station and huge conduits running for miles across valleys and
burrowing through hills, though they are probably buried in the earth by
now. Actually they were large enough to drive a jeep through and are used
to drain water in enormous quantities from the Sea of Galilee, to irrigate
arid areas to the south.

While we must regret the passing of old Biblical landmarks after all
these centuries, still we must agree that the needs of the present take
precedence over the sacred memorials of the past. Not far from the place
where Jesus Christ made His immortal statements about the water of life,
Galilee water in great volume will roar through conduits the like of which
the Romans never saw.

It could be that in time many existing evidences of historical Biblical civilization may be modified or even erased. Of course, Mount Hermon will still brood over the land. And Mount Tabor will continue to raise its rounded dome over the plain of Esdraelon or Armageddon, and may we hope that a portion of the Sea of Galilee will remain to remind us of the immortal teachings of love and brotherhood once proclaimed on its banks.

It would seem, however, that Nazareth has not changed too much in the nearly 2,000 years of the Christian era, except to grow larger. The tall green cypresses and flat white roofs of houses have timeless qualities that seem little affected by the modern world. The dry, sun-baked, boulder-strewn hillsides, the presence of donkeys as a form of transport, and the extremities of heat would probably seem familiar if the ancients were to return. For us the chief meaning of Nazareth is that it was the place from which Jesus Christ went out to fulfill the great mission of His life.

Personally I find the holy places in Nazareth somewhat less than satisfying, and indeed so crass were the local guides on my recent trips that I have taken to avoiding the usual sights altogether. If I go into the town at all, it is to visit the old synagogue in which it is said Jesus read the Scriptures and taught, and from which the angry congregation took Him to the "hill of precipitation" to throw Him over, the same hill now being used as a stone quarry.

I like to sit in this barren little synagogue and imagine the graciousness with which He read words that symbolized His ministry. "The spirit of the Lord is upon me, because he hath anointed me to preach the gospel to the poor; he hath sent me to heal the brokenhearted, to preach deliverance to the captives, and recovering of sight to the blind, to set at liberty them that are bruised . . . And he closed the book . . . and the eyes of all them that were in the synagogue were fastened on him." (Luke 4:18-20) And we might add, the eyes of all mankind have been fastened on Him ever since. For He has fascinated men in all centuries. That, incidentally, is why we are here in the Holy Land, because He fascinates us also. Beyond visiting this old synagogue I like to sit upon the terrace of the charming Grand New Hotel on the heights above the town and meditate in the lovely environment He knew so well. I find it intriguing to realize that He looked at these same hills and gazed over the far stretching valley of Jezreel.

From Nazareth to Tiberias is only 19½ miles, which gives some idea of the miniature distances in this country and the restricted geographical compass of Jesus' activities. On our way to the Sea of Galilee we pass through Kefar-Kana (Cana) where Jesus performed His first miracle in which He

Tiberias on the Sea of Galilee has the Syrian shore as a background.

turned water into wine. (John 2:1-11) Vilnay quotes a pilgrim, Antoninus Martyr, who is said to have visited Cana in A.D. 570, "where our Lord was at the wedding, and we reclined upon His very couch, upon which I, unworthy that I am, wrote the names of my parents." (This I would say proves nothing about a couch still intact after 543 years, but does prove that even back in A.D. 570 boys were boys." In the old church at Cana a priest solemnly showed me a jar said to be the very one used in the miracle. We looked at each other without the flicker of an eyelash.

The road now circles the lower Galilee, traversing a lovely countryside rich in memories of Jesus. I have always experienced a peaceful feeling while passing through this area; the wind stirs the cypress trees and over all is the golden sunshine. Field after field of sunflowers line the road, the great flowers solemnly bowing their heads when the sun declines.

It is believed this is the region where Jesus and His disciples, while passing through the fertile cornfields on the Sabbath, plucked the corn and ate it, to the horror of the Pharisees who complained that this act violated Sabbath laws. But Jesus reminded them that when David was hungry he also ignored such laws, and that stopped them. Anyway, as He said to them, "The Sabbath was made for man, and not man for the Sabbath: Therefore the Son of man is Lord also of the sabbath." (Mark 2:27-28)

Finally we see in noble panorama the immortal Sea of Galilee lying in a great cup 680 feet below sea level. How many times Jesus must have stopped on this height to look at the lake He loved so dearly. The great expanse of blue water is surrounded by brown hills, and shimmers in the soft heat haze of the summer afternoon. The sea is 13 miles long, its greatest width 8 miles, its circumference 32⅓ miles, its greatest depth about 200 feet.

We descend quickly into Tiberias, a city built by Herod Antipas and named in honor of the reigning emperor. Built on the edge of an ancient walled town called Rakkatk, whose cemetery lies beneath it, Tiberias was shunned by pious Jews in Jesus' time. The city is mentioned only once in the Gospels: "There came other boats from Tiberias nigh unto the place where they did eat bread, after that the Lord had given thanks." (John 6:23)

We go at once to the Galei Kinnereth Hotel, a pleasant hostelry and indeed a favorite stopping place of ours, which is ideally situated directly on the shore of the sea. What an unforgettable pleasure to sit on the terrace and to watch the sun go down over the Syrian hills across the Sea of Galilee. Across the lake is the place where Jesus commanded the demons to come out of the man who wandered among the tombs and where the swine rushed down a slope into the sea. (Matt. 8:28-32)

At dinner we dine on Peter's fish, so-called because the Galilean musht or comb fish found in the sea is similar in characteristics to a fish pictured in a Second-Century mosaic discovered nearby. This is very likely a type of fish caught in these same waters by Simon Peter. There is another explanation why it is called Peter's fish; legend says that it was from the mouth of this fish that Peter took the tribute money.

After dinner we rest for a while under the large eucalyptus trees growing through the floor of this terrace. The moon rises over the hills of Syria, mounting higher into the star-studded sky until at last it sends a long path of silver across the beloved sea that since childhood has been enshrined in our spiritual heritage. As the water gently laps the pebbly shore the lovely words of an old, old hymn come to mind:

> O Sabbath rest by Galilee!
> O calm of hills above!
> Where Jesus knelt to share with Thee
> The silence of eternity,
> Interpreted by love.

It is on this steep bank by the seashore where it is believed Jesus commanded the demons to come out of an afflicted man and where the swine rushed down a slope into the sea. (Matt. 9:28-32)

20

Walking with Jesus in Galilee

ITHIN THE SPACE OF ONLY TEN MILES, THAT IS TO SAY, THE DIS-
tance from Tiberias to Capernaum, the world received
its deepest wisdom and its greatest spiritual truth. For
within the compass of these few miles the Sermon on the Mount was
preached, the feeding of the 5,000 took place, the sermon was delivered
from the boat, the calling of the disciples occurred. Acts of love and healing
were performed that have moved and softened the heart of humanity for
twenty centuries.

I have been up and down this shoreline several times with my good
friend Reuben Ben Dori, who lives on the heights above Tiberias; and to
whose knowledge of this area and to whose kindly spirit I am gratefully
indebted.

As we take the road along the sea, we notice little fishing boats anchored
off the shore, and nets drying in the sun, after the fashion of olden times.
Soon we come to a mound marked Magdala. This is the site of an important town of antiquity, noteworthy as the home of one of the most
famous courtesans of history, a woman fair of form and face, known as Mary
of Magdala. There is a spring nearby which for many centuries has bubbled
hot out of the hillside into a basin called "Mary's pool." According to
tradition, Mary of Magdala came here to bathe in the hot waters that were
supposed to enhance beauty.

Despite her great beauty, there was no happiness in this woman, conflicted as she was, not merely by one, but by "seven devils." She suffered
from "evil spirits and infirmities," the latter probably referring subtly to

Mary's pool at ancient Magdala is a warm spring which has been flowing for centuries. Here Mary Magdalene came to bathe on the supposition that the waters contained a beauty-enhancing power.

lesions within the soul and in the emotional structure of her nature. She was the unhappy victim of a too-beautiful face and body.

But one day in this very area Mary met a Man Who fixed His eyes upon her as no man had ever looked at her before. His level gaze ignored her body and penetrated to the essence of her mind, to the inner depths of the soul that no one had ever seen or even thought about. He was not unaware of the profoundly tangled complexities of her conflicted mind, a condition that in our time might well require the services of the most astute psychiatrist. This woman's sickness lay deeply imbedded, the profound typing of which is colorfully indicated by the description of extreme possession by multiple demons.

But the Man Who studied this unhappy human being was no ordinary healer. The vast powers of God were available to Him. His healing forces were powerfully projected upon this illness, and the astonishing miracle of healing took place. Luke, himself a physician who realized the extraordinary quality of this cure, reports the case history simply: "And certain women, which had been healed of evil spirits and infirmities, Mary called Magdalene, out of whom went seven devils." (Luke 8:2) Only Jesus could have done this wonderful thing, but He could and did. The extent of the change in her is attested by the fact that in the garden of the resurrection she was the first to meet Him after He rose from the dead.

We are traveling now through the land of Gennesaret, where Jesus preached and healed the sick. Indeed, He was so sought after by the multitudes of sick and needy people and by the many who were always uplifted by His words that it was often necessary to retire to the other side of the lake or into the mountains. But whenever He returned to the land of Gennesaret they again flocked around Him.

Mark (6:53-56) describes the oft-repeated scene: "And when they had passed over, they came into the land of Gennesaret, and drew to the shore. And when they were come out of the ship, straightway they knew Him.

And ran through the whole region round about, and began to carry about in beds those that were sick, where they heard he was. And whithersoever he entered, into village, or cities, or country, they laid the sick in the streets, and besought him that they might touch if it were but the border of his garment: and as many as touched him were made whole."

In fact, there was one place, and we come there now, where there is a cove in the shoreline not far from the road where Jesus was forced to get into a boat and push off a few feet from shore, so great was the crowd. He spoke to the people from the boat, the big crowd sitting on the grassy hillside. Luke (5:1-3) tells us: "And it came to pass, that, as the people pressed upon him to hear the word of God, he stood by the lake of Gennesaret, and saw two ships standing by the lake: but the fishermen were gone out of them, and were washing their nets. And He entered into one of the ships, which was Simon's, and prayed him that he would thrust out a little from the land. And He sat down, and taught the people out of the ship."

It must have been very effective as a speaking place, for the terrain acts as a natural amphitheater and sounding board, for the acoustics is so perfect that the voice carries far and clearly. A minister from America actually demonstrated the acoustical properties of the place to a large crowd of pilgrims, himself speaking from a boat.

Presently we come to Tabgha, to the Church of the Multiplication of Loaves and Fish, so called because it marks the spot where Jesus fed the five thousand with five loaves and two fishes. H. V. Morton believes the place of the feeding of the 5,000 is farther on at the site of Bethsaida-Julias, and that this church is a memorial of the event.

In the same neighborhood rises a lovely hill with gentle slopes which has been known for centuries as the Mount of the Beatitudes. A convent stands on its summit, and in the serene arches of its colonnade one may dream and meditate while looking down upon the slope stretching to the

In this cove along the Galilean shore, Jesus preached from a boat to a crowd seated on the gentle hillside. The contour of sea and land gives the spot a perfect natural sound-effect. (Luke 5:1-3)

water's edge. We may easily reconstruct the scene when a vast audience sat here listening spellbound to the words of wisdom, to the majestic and perfect phraseology that fell from the lips of the Nazarene.

Deeply impressed as they were, these listeners could not have known that the words they were hearing that day would live and be venerated forever as the most priceless speech of all time. How could they know that civilizations yet unborn and thousands of miles from that grassy hillside would be based upon immortal words of the Sermon on the Mount? We listen carefully and prayerfully in the still morning air. What did His voice sound like? Surely it must have been at once gentle and strong, reaching our ears and our hearts and minds with the ringing quality of a silver bell. What an inestimable privilege to have heard Him say in this very place: "Blessed are the poor in spirit: for theirs is the kingdom of heaven. Blessed are they that mourn: for they shall be comforted. . . . Blessed are the pure in heart: for they shall see God." (Matt. 5:3-12)

This place stimulates deeper than ordinary reflection, and in meditating upon the great speech made here, we are amazed that a simple, unschooled Teacher could think and enunciate principles that have not only survived but also greatly surpassed the writings of the world's most erudite men. How to account for it? Only that He was the Son of God and therefore in profounder contact with ultimate truth than any other man who has ever lived on this earth.

The speech outlines the kind of people who are blessed, and holds forth the hard fact that those who suffer for being righteous, that is the good and right-minded, will experience even deeper blessing. He shows that such people illuminate the whole world as lights that cannot be hid. He makes it clear that He did not come to destroy ancient spiritual law, but to give it deeper and more meaningful application; in other words, to universalize it into timeless usage. He proceeds to elevate the principle of love as the solution to all relationships both personal and within the group. Rconciliation and understanding are the fruits of such love and this, of course, holds within it the potential of peace and brotherhood.

The subtlety of Jesus' perception is revealed in His treatment of adultery, for example. He indicates that not merely is it the act that is sinful, but thoughts of a lustful nature are equally sinful. Indeed, thought is not only the ancestor of a deed, but also lust in the thoughts corrodes the soul, and so hurtful is any kind of sin that even the eye that transmits the thought to the brain had better be gouged out than to continue to nurse evil thoughts. This is so subtle that no one had ever made it clear before, and indeed it is at the bottom of much emotional difficulty of today.

On this slope overlooking the Sea of Galilee, a great congregation heard Jesus preach the Sermon on the Mount.

He proceeds to demolish the long-established eye-for-an-eye, tooth-for-a-tooth, you-hit-me-and-I-will-hit-you doctrine—the stupid policy that has kept the world and people in an uproar through all time. The wise principle of turning the other cheek was so revolutionary that it must have surprised and bewildered those who sat on this hillside listening. Even now we write it off as unworkable. You may recall H. G. Wells' famous comment, "Is it any wonder that to this day this Galilean is too much for our small hearts." But those who really try His teachings are rewarded with the deep peace and blessing they bestow and the spiritual growth they stimulate.

It goes without saying that the principles Jesus taught on this grassy slope fronting the deep blue, sparkling lake are demanding. Indeed, the theologian Reinhold Niebuhr calls the whole speech an "impossible possibility," meaning that since men are human it is extremely difficult to attain the standard of love advocated by the Master. But this, of course, does not mean that we should not try. Besides, we have available to us the grace of God which supplies strength we do not possess on the basis of our human nature alone.

Apparently Jesus Himself realized what He was asking of those people trained for long centuries to hate their enemies. Discipleship of Him required a profound change of attitude so that they could actually love their enemies and pray for those who mistreated them. At this, some startled listener on the hillside must have held up his hand. "Question please, Master. Wouldn't what you are saying mean that we have to be perfect, and what man can be that?" But this did not cause Jesus to retreat at all. He told them that the ideal of perfection must be held. He stoutly declared, "Be ye therefore perfect, even as your Father which is in heaven is perfect." (Matt. 5:48)

He really took apart the hypocrites and stuffed shirts who put on a religious show to fool others and themselves, too. And He had something to say about complicated prayers and involved liturgies. He taught the people a simple, direct prayer. I wonder what the Master would think were He to return physically and listen to the pious rigmarole that some services of Christian worship have become under the liturgical experts to whom the subtle power of simplicity seems completely foreign. He actually told people to get rid of the sour looks which they used to indicate piety. His church has indeed done a pretty doubtful job of living up to this marvelous sermon preached from this mount where we now sit.

He takes care of money-grabbing, and must have had a perceptive, long view of market crashes and depressions in which treasures proved indeed unsure and insecure. But those who were smart enough to accumulate spiritual treasure could ride out any storm, so He urged the people "to let go and let God," and to put their faith in that which you *can* take with you. And another subtle thought was to live for today and not wear yourself sick worrying about tomorrow. Lots of His followers should make a special study of this point.

And don't go around judging people, trying to make them over in your own image, He says. Just get busy and get yourself straightened out. God is good and God loves you, He told the people. So if you truly ask and seek and knock, the door will be opened and you will receive. All of which seems to lay emphasis upon the wonderful flow of blessings that will come to the simple, trusting souls who become as little children; in whom there is no super-duper sophistication, no know-it-all attitude. He realized how very hard all this was that He was saying, for He acknowledged that ". . . strait is the gate, and narrow is the way, which leadeth unto life, and few there be that find it." (Matt. 7:14) But He also said in a powerful conclusion to His sermon that "Whosoever heareth these sayings of mine, and doeth them, I will liken him unto a wise man, which built his house

Arched colonnade of the convent standing serenely on the Mount of Beatitudes overlooks the sea and the scene of the Sermon on the Mount.

upon a rock: And the rain descended, and the floods came, and the winds blew, and beat upon that house; and it fell not: for it was founded upon a rock. And every one that heareth these sayings of mine, and doeth them not, shall be likened unto a foolish man, which built his house upon the sand: And the rain descended, and the flood came, and the winds blew, and beat upon that house; and it fell: and great was the fall of it." (Matt. 7:24-27)

When He ended His remarks the crowd sat spellbound, astonished, for the authority with which He spoke was unmistakable. He had the truth, and this fact communicated itself to the big crowd that heard Him that day on the green slopes above the shining water. And that astonishment continues to this present time. Indeed, that is one reason we are here re-thinking and re-praying the wonderful truth which He taught on the Mount and by the Sea of Galilee.

Mosaic showing a basket of loaves is flanked by fish in the floor of the Church of the Multiplication (of loaves and fish). Date is supposed to be Second or Third Century. The same type of fish as pictured here is still caught in the Sea of Galilee.

21

The Trip of a Lifetime
Draws to a Close

AS WE CONTINUE IN THE FOOTSTEPS OF OUR MASTER ALONG THIS
lovely lakeshore where He performed so many of His mighty
works and taught immortal lessons for us all, we come to a
meaningful place. A church stands here called Saint Peter's Church and it
is built over a great rock, a rock that has considerable significance.

To me it is comforting and encouraging to visit this place for it was here
that a weak man was made strong—very strong. And the great thing is that
all men who have failed our Lord are here reminded that Jesus can make
rocklike characters of us also. For Jesus Christ is the Saviour of men today
no less than in the yesterdays.

This was one of the locations where the risen Christ revealed Himself to
His disciples after His resurrection. Seven of the disciples were fishing out
on the lake in the gray dawn when Christ, having risen from the dead, appeared on the shore. He called to them across the water but they failed to
recognize him, seeing only a lone figure standing beneath the trees that
fringed the water's edge.

Again they heard a clear ringing voice: "Children, have ye any meat?"
(John 21:5-7) "No," came back the answer. Then something in the way
the Stranger carried Himself and the accents of a beloved voice got through
to John. He cried excitedly to Peter, "It is the Lord!"

That was all that Peter needed. Forthright character that he was, he
grabbed up his coat to cover himself, being naked at his work, and not
waiting for the ship to come ashore leaped into the sea. His powerful arms
brought him quickly to land. The other disciples brought the ship in, its
dragging nets filled with fish.

157

St. Peter's Church stands over this rock. Built of black basalt stones, it marks the site where Jesus revealed Himself to His disciples after the resurrection as they fished in the early morning. Perhaps this could have been the rock Jesus had in mind when He said, "Upon this rock I will build my church; and the gates of hell shall not prevail against it." (Matt. 16:18)

On shore they found a fire laid and fish cooking. Bread also was ready for the hungry men. Then Jesus invited them to breakfast. Perhaps they ate on some of these dark basalt stones we see here. And that big rock under the nearby church may have been in the mind of Jesus who had, of course, seen it so many times when He had said to Peter up by Caesarea Philippi: " . . . upon this rock I will build my church; and the gates of hell shall not prevail against it." (Matt. 16:18)

But poor Peter had proved far from rocklike. And he could not help timidly wondering, as they sat down for breakfast that morning, just how Jesus did feel toward him. He was not long in discovering the wonderful fact that Jesus had completely forgiven him for his denial. Jesus knew a real man and was well aware that Peter had passed through the fire and could now be counted on. He had become rocklike indeed through the redemptive power of Christ.

The breakfast gathering was just like old times despite the incredible fact that since they were last together in this way their Master had actually been killed and His body placed in a tomb. But now here He was alive, cooking fish over a fire and eating fish and bread for the nourishment of an obviously physical body. After breakfast they sat in the cool morning air watching the sun breaking across the Syrian hills and being glad that the old band was together again.

Jesus sat studying this man Peter. The big, bearded fellow meant so very much to Him. Quietly He asked, "Simon, son of Jonas, lovest thou me more than these?" (John 21:15) Startled, Peter exclaimed with the same old impulsiveness, "Yea, Lord; thou knowest that I love thee." Jesus replied, "Feed my lambs," meaning that he was to carry the message to people everywhere and to feed them spiritually.

Twice again He asked the same penetrating question and in both instances received the same sincere positive answer of love and devotion. This scene is full of wonder, for these three strong affirmations made by Peter canceled out his three previous pathetic denials.

Here, where this wonderful cancellation took place, we are reminded that our own denials may likewise be canceled out by His Grace. Our weaknesses may also be transmuted into rocklike qualities.

We arrive now at Capernaum. I shall never forget the first time I walked through this grove of eucalyptus trees into the ruins of "His own city." I found myself choking up and my eyes filling with tears. Jesus seemed so very near, for surely He still loves this spot on the shore of the Sea of Galilee as He loved it in the long ago.

Capernaum is the scene of some of the most wonderful healings of Jesus, and as one walks these roads it is not too difficult to visualize how the crowds loved Him and wanted to touch Him. Here He healed the daughter of Jairus and the servant of a centurion. Here He healed Peter's mother-in-law, whom, no doubt, He knew well, for He was often a guest in Peter's house (the ruins of which can still be seen). Here also He healed the maniac, the man with the withered hand and the blind man whom He cured on the Sabbath day.

It was also in Capernaum that a poor woman, suffering from an abnormal issue of blood for years and not finding help in her trouble, crept timidly through the crowd and on touching the bottom of the Master's garment was healed. And that charming incident took place here when those people who had so much faith, yet were unable to reach the Master because of the crowds, ingeniously let the sick man down through a roof to the feet of Jesus Who healed him.

So here indeed in Capernaum is where the glorious healing ministry of Jesus reached its peak. The Scriptures tell us "the whole multitude sought to touch him: for there went virtue out of him, and healed them all." (Luke 6:19) And bear in mind this important fact: Jesus Christ still heals even in this modern world for He is "Jesus Christ the same yesterday, and today, and forever." (Heb. 13:8)

Time has, of course, wrought vast changes not only in Capernaum but also along the entire Galilean shore. The hills now barren of vegetation were once covered with a growth of trees. It could be that much forest destruction is traceable to the Romans and later to the 400-year Turkish occupation of Palestine when, in both instances, trees were ruthlessly taken for military purposes; and no doubt the forested hills attracted more rainfall than falls at present. Ancient aqueducts, the ruins of which can be seen in various locations, would appear to bear out this assumption.

The crowds (numbering up to 5,000 people, according to Gospel record) that were attracted to the sermons of Jesus bear out the belief that the shore of Galilee was a busy one in ancient times. Also, the level of the Sea of Galilee may be higher now than in the past. One day while lunching at Ein Gev I met an archaeologist who spoke of pavements and of a Roman galleon tied up underwater off Magdala. He thought the early town was more extensive than had been presumed, and extended into what is now the lake bed.

From all that we can learn, Capernaum itself might have had a population of perhaps 15,000 or 20,000—a large community for those times. It was cosmopolitan in character since trade routes from Tyre and Sidon to Damascus, and between Antioch and Jerusalem, centered here. And so its streets were filled with a mixture of Jews, Romans, Greeks, Egyptians and Bedouins. In this quiet place of today it is difficult to imagine the busy commerce and shipping that once existed here. There were places of amusement, also. Prostitution, one of man's most ancient social festers, no doubt flourished as did other forms of vice. It was altogether a thriving, roaring and often sinful center of life; and since Jesus always went where human need was greatest, He spent much of His ministry in this city and adjacent territory. His message of love and salvation encountered the strong resistance of sin and evil in Capernaum and in neighboring Chorazin and Bethsaida, and He had some stern unminced words to say:

> Woe unto thee, Chorazin: woe unto thee, Bethsaida: for if the mighty works, which were done in you, had been done in Tyre and Sidon, they would have repented long ago in sackcloth and ashes. But I say unto you, it shall be more tolerable for Tyre and Sidon at the day of judgment, than for you. And thou, Capernaum, which art exalted unto heaven, shalt be brought down to hell: for if the mighty works, which have been done in thee, had been done in Sodom, it would have remained until this day. But I say unto you, That it shall be more tolerable for the land of Sodom in the day of judgment, than for thee. (Matt. 11:21-24)

The chief object of interest in Capernaum today is the glorious ruin of what must have been an extraordinary beautiful synagogue which some authorities say seated approximately 1,500 people. Even in their fallen

In these ruins of the magnificent synagogue at Capernaum, Jesus may have preached. It is an extraordinarily beautiful structure with exquisite carving and symbolism.

state the stones and capitals are exquisite in their carving and symbolism, and show a charm and artistic beauty indicative of Greek and Roman influences. It is possible that in this very building Jesus spoke, and His eyes may have delighted in the beautiful sculpturing we see carved on these ancient stones. Perhaps these very columns echoed to the melodic sound of His voice. Indeed it may have been in this very place that He uttered those great words that have blessed so many, "I am the bread of life: he that cometh to Me shall never hunger; and he that believeth on Me shall never thirst." (John 6:35)

A Franciscan Father showed me a stone that, because of its shape, may have formed part of the chair of the Preacher. Could Jesus actually have sat upon this stone? Who knows! But one thing is sure: the great things He said and did on this spot have vitally affected our lives and it is this fact that has brought us reverently to this place.

I have often wandered along the shoreline, trying to mark out the ancient quayside which, because of the size of the ancient city, must have extended some distance into what now is open country; but which in the time of Jesus was a busy section of the portside within the city's bounds. I had read how H. V. Morton had seen several huge heart-shaped stones which, from the marks made on them by fishermen's grappling irons, might be considered part of the quay of ancient Capernaum. I very much wanted to see these stones and whether I found the exact ones to which Morton referred is not certain. I did feel that I satisfied my desire to stand on the site where "Matthew, sitting at the receipt of custom" (Matt. 9:9) was called to follow Christ. The calling of Matthew has always been for me one of the great incidents in the Galilean ministry of our Lord.

Matthew was one of the hated publicans whose job under the Romans was to collect all the taxes and fees that the traffic would bear. Merchandise coming in by caravan or by water was subject to duty. Every farthing that might possibly be extracted was taken from the people, so that the tax-gatherer was soundly hated. We may believe that Matthew, being in on the politician's racket, got his own cut both by deal and by failure to report everything he took in. So he sat here every day by the quayside where he could very well watch the life of the town while he raked in the cash. No doubt he had often seen Jesus pass by always followed by throngs, and it is not unlikely that Matthew's interest was piqued so that he, too, listened to the fascinating Teacher and evidently was himself intrigued. Jesus was getting to him more than he realized. The seeds of new life had been planted within him.

I have always imagined that Matthew had a yen for gold. As he sat at the custom place he might have delighted in letting the Roman eagles which he collected run lovingly through his fingers. I have held such a coin in my own hand and its patina is very soft and smooth, its inscription clear and distinct despite all the centuries since it was minted.

So, on that day of unsuspected destiny, here sat Matthew at his booth reveling in his gold, when suddenly a shadow fell over his desk. He looked up into the eyes of a Man. The Man looked searchingly into the eyes of the taxgatherer—he who had such a profitable racket. The gaze was long and direct. Jesus saw behind the outer personality a real man and Matthew glimpsed a greater life mirrored in those eyes. Then Jesus spoke, saying simply, "Follow me," And Matthew who writes his own one-verse auto-biography (Matt. 9:9) said, "And he arose, and followed him."

The golden eagles fell unheeded from the taxgatherer's fingers; the hoarded money was forgotten. He got up immediately, leaving everything and unhesitatingly followed this wonderful Person. What an extremely remarkable personality Jesus was: merely to say the word and at once a tough man walks away from graft and wealth. The power of Jesus Christ to draw strong, tough men, and bind them to Him is dramatically illustrated in this astonishing incident that occurred right here on this quayside.

But Jesus more than compensated Matthew for his loss of gold by giving him a "golden" pen with which he wrote that immortal document, known and beloved by millions, The Gospel According to St. Matthew.

The extraordinary effect Jesus had upon men, motivating them to give up everything to follow Him, is illustrated in the case of others. Walking by the seaside in the early days of His ministry He saw two men: brothers named Simon, also called Peter, and Andrew (Matt. 4:18-22). They were casting nets out of their boat into the sea even as fishermen do today in the very same waters.

Jesus called out to them: "Follow me, and I will make you fishers of men." And what did they do? Wave their hands amusedly and say, "Go away, we have our job to do"? Not at all. "They straightaway left their nets, and followed him."

One thing is sure; no soft super-nice character, as some people mistakenly regard Jesus, could be so compelling a leader of men.

The same thing occurred when He came to the firm of Zebedee and Sons, large-scale fish handlers of Capernaum. Men were hard at work mending their nets in a ship just offshore when Jesus came along and called the two sons to join Him in His great spiritual enterprise. "And they immediately left the ship and their father, and followed Him." (Matt. 4:22)

We can only imagine how the father liked this, but perhaps he figured that working with the famous Teacher would mean a lot more to his boys, James and John, than the fishing business, and he was willing to carry on by himself. It could even be that the ambitious Mrs. Zebedee had something to do with it. Later she actually tried to get her two sons appointed to the main posts in the type of kingdom she, in her ambition, thought Jesus had in mind. She wanted Him to "Grant that these my two sons may sit, the one on thy right hand, and the other on the left, in thy kingdom." (Matthew 20:21)

But Jesus set her straight, calling her attention to the suffering His followers would endure and saying that only God could assign positions in the spiritual kingdom. He also pointed out that great positions would only go to humble servants of God. Despite this try of a doting mother these two boys proved themselves real disciples. They turned out to be strong men. They kept the faith to the end of their lives, and a bitter end it was.

One day when we stopped to rest awhile by the seaside, we turned to the New Testament and read aloud that wonderful story of the storm at sea and the stilling of the waters. We had noticed that the wind had increased and whitecaps dotted the water. "Wouldn't it be great if we could actually see a storm on the Sea of Galilee?" someone said. Almost in answer to our wish the sudden storm increased in intensity until the lake was whipped up into a small fury. The waters that had turned greenish were angrily frothing with spray and spume.

It was an unforgettable conclusion to our visit, for it brought vividly to mind the Galilean storm and dramatic experience described by St. Matthew! "And when he was entered into a ship, his disciples followed him. And, behold, there arose a great tempest in the sea, insomuch that the ship was covered with the waves; but he was asleep." (Matt. 8:23-24)

What a picture! What a Person! No fear, no terror. A perfect Man of nature, a perfect Man of God. What a demonstration of poise, mental health, full vigorous manhood. There He lay peacefully sleeping, rocked in the cradle of the deep.

But not so the disciples. They were hardy men and they knew the sea. But this storm was different. Its violence lifted the boat up on one gigantic wave, only to let it slide sickeningly into the trough of the next. The wind whistled through the spars and howled in fury, and these men with blanched faces expected any moment to be their last. And there in the midst of the cataclysm of sound and tempest lay the Master sleeping peacefully.

They cried out to Him in their terror, "Lord, save us: we perish."

Slowly Jesus opened His eyes and deliciously stretched His athletic body. He looked round at the fearful faces circling Him. With a gentle smile He said, "Why are ye fearful, O ye of little faith?" (Matt. 8:25-26)

Slowly He arose, walking across the deck of the pitching vessel, sloshing through the water that had shipped aboard. He steadied Himself with one arm around the mast. The flying spray drenched Him to the skin and the wind tossed His hair in the stiff breeze. Then He raised His right hand high and His magnificent voice rang out over the raging waters. "Peace, be still." There was a moment of hesitation as mighty nature was rebuked by the mighty Son of God. And then "the wind ceased, and there was a great calm." (Mark 4:39)

We must now take to the road for a quick trip to the airport at Tel Aviv. The road winds for miles around beautiful Mount Tabor, which is said to be the Biblical Mount of Transfiguration.

Enroute we pass Endor, scene of a dramatic Old Testament story. Endor was an important town when King Saul camped in nearby Mount Gilboa preparing to fight the Philistines. But Saul became frightened when he saw the huge host the Philistines had brought up against him. So he went to consult a woman soothsayer or clairvoyant at Endor. She communicated with Samuel who was dead and gave Saul the sad news that he, too, was to die. (I Sam. 28:5-25)

Mount Tabor (1,843 feet above sea level) is considered to be the Mount of Transfiguration. (Matt. 17:1-9) From its summit is a magnificent vista of the Jezreel Valley. To the south may be seen the mountains of Samaria extending into Carmel to the west and Gilboa to the east. The snowy summit of Mount Hermon is also seen, recalling the words of the psalmist, "The north and the south thou hast created them; Tabor and Hermon shall rejoice in Thy name." (Psalm 89:12)

Our route also takes us by the village of Nain, which is situated across a little plain on a hillside. It was here that Jesus came once with His disciples and found a funeral procession at the gate of the city. It seems that a widow's only son had died. The mother and son must have been greatly liked, for a large number of people accompanied the body. The mother was, of course, grief-stricken and Jesus out of His great heart of love had compassion on her. He touched the bier upon which the young man's body lay "and he that was dead sat up, and began to speak. And He delivered him to his mother." (Luke 7:11-15) We ride on thinking of Jesus and the love He had, and has, for sorrowing humanity.

Through these pages we have walked where Jesus walked. Now we are once again in a modern airport. Our great jet is ready and we step aboard. Down the runway we gather speed and take off over fields where the Master once walked. Quickly we are in the air, and the plane points its nose westward. Looking down, we are passing over the coastline at Caesarea. We can make out the ancient jetty from which both Paul and Peter shipped West, carrying the blessed Gospel of Salvation. In a moment the Holy Land falls away behind us, but for a thousand miles we fly over islands and lands where St. Paul journeyed and built the Church in the long ago and about which we hope to write in another book.

As we fly swiftly westward in this great airplane, symbol of a modern civilization, we pray that as disciples of Jesus we may help strengthen and deepen the Christian faith in the life of our time. The trip of a lifetime challenges us to the service of a lifetime.

Bibliography

Albright, W. F. *The Archaeology of Palestine*. Baltimore: Penguin Books, 1961.

Allegro, J. M. *The Dead Sea Scrolls*. Baltimore: Penguin Books, 1959.

Antonius, George. *The Arab Awakening*. Philadelphia: Lippincott, 1939.

Byng, Edward J. *The World of the Arabs*. Boston: Little, Brown, 1944.

Fosdick, Harry Emerson. *A Pilgrimage to Palestine*. New York: Macmillan, 1927.

Haddad, George. *History of Baalbek*. Lebanon: Mustafa Ibrehim Al-Jamal & Sons, 1961.

Harris, George L. *Jordan—Its People—Its Society—Its Culture*. New York: Grove Press, 1958.

Hitti, Philip K. *History of the Arabs*. New York: Macmillan, 1951.

———. *The Arabs—A Short History*. Princeton, New Jersey: Princeton University Press, 1943.

Keller, Werner. *The Bible As History*. New York: Morrow, 1961.

Kenyon, Kathleen M. *Digging Up Jericho*. New York: Praeger, 1957.

Landau, Rom. *The Arab Heritage of Western Civilization*. New York: Arab Information Center, 1962.

Miller, Madeleine S. and J. Lane. *Encyclopedia of Bible Life*. New York: Harper, 1955.

———. *Harper's Bible Dictionary*. New York: Harper, 1961.

Morton, H. V. *In the Steps of the Master*. New York: Dodd, Mead, 1959.

Nasir, Sari Jamil. *The Image of the Arab in American Popular Culture*. Urbana, Graduate College of the University of Illinois, 1962.

Payne, Melvin M. "75 Years Exploring Earth, Sea, and Sky," *National Geographic Magazine*, Vol. 123, No. 1, January 1963.

Pritchard, James B. *Archaeology and the Old Testament*. Princeton, New Jersey: Princeton University Press, 1958.

———. *Gibeon, Where the Sun Stood Still*. Princeton, New Jersey: Princeton University Press, 1962.

Slaughter, Frank G. *The Land and the Promise*. New York: World Pub. Co., 1960.

Smith, George Adam. *The Historical Georgraphy of the Holy Land*. London: Hodder and Stoughton.

Thomson, W. M. *The Land and the Book*. New York: Harper, 1860.

Vester, Bertha Spafford. *Our Jerusalem—An American Family in the Holy City, 1881-1949*. Lebanon: Middle East Export Press, Inc., 1950.

Vilnay, Zev. *The Guide to Israel*. Jerusalem, Israel: Central Press, 1961.

Weatherhead, Leslie D. *It Happened in Palestine*. Nashville, Tenn.: Abingdon Press, 1936.

Index

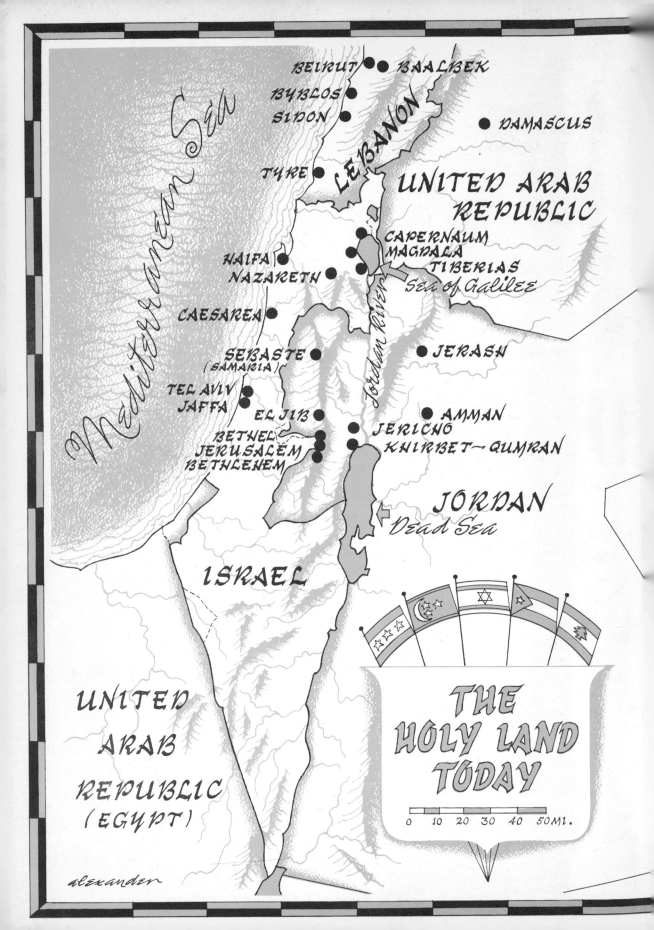

THE SCRIPTURES ARE A GREAT TREASURE

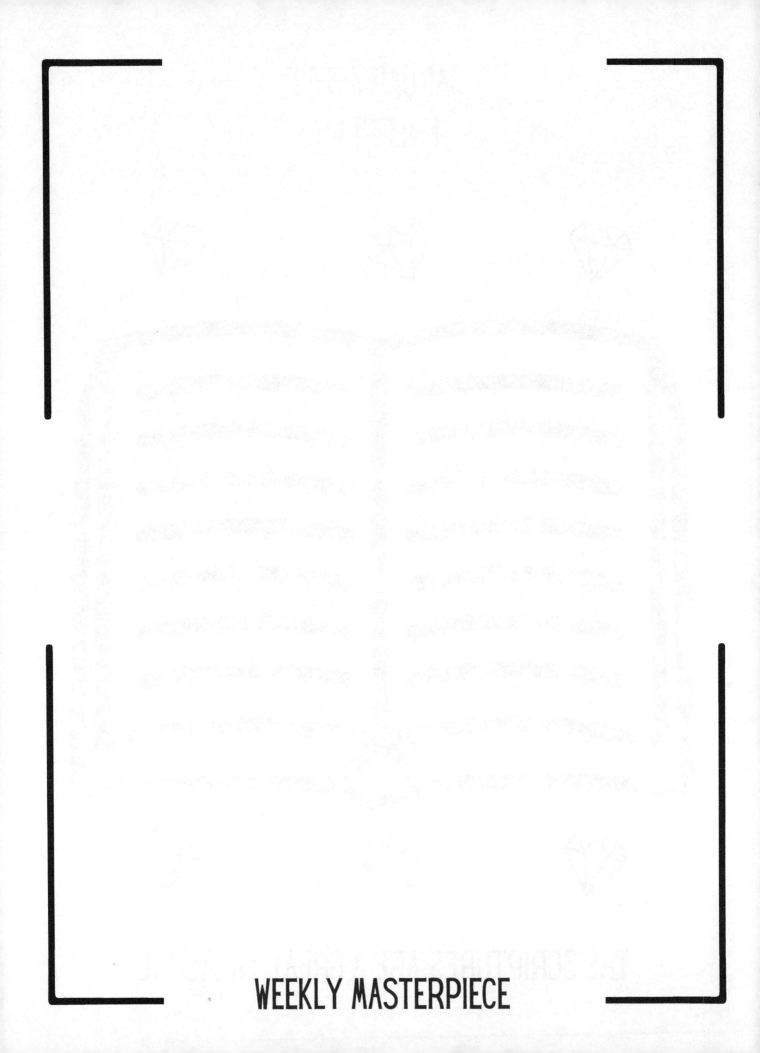

WEEKLY MASTERPIECE

JANUARY 15-21
1 NEPHI 6-10

I CAN HOLD ONTO
THE IRON ROD

WEEKLY MASTERPIECE